TACKLE S

GW00363808

Tackle Snooker

JOHN PULMAN

STANLEY PAUL
London

STANLEY PAUL & CO. LTD

3 Fitzroy Square, London W1

An imprint of the Hutchinson Publishing Group

London Melbourne Sydney Auckland
Wellington Johannesburg Cape Town
and agencies throughout the world

First published 1965
Revised edition 1974

Printed in Great Britain by The Anchor Press Ltd
and bound by Wm Brendon & Son Ltd
both of Tiptree, Essex

ISBN 0 09 121270 7 (cased)
0 09 121271 5 (paper)

Contents

CONTENTS

Introduction

Snooker is played as widely, perhaps more widely, than any other indoor game in this country yet, curiously it produces a smaller percentage of good players than most others.

The actual method of play is very easily grasped. It can be explained to anyone in a few minutes. Snooker is played on a billiards table with twenty-two balls, comprising fifteen reds and six colours—yellow, green, brown, blue, pink and black—and the cue ball (white). The latter is the only ball that can be struck with the cue. All the scoring is by potting and the mode of play is to pot a red and a colour alternately.

Reds stay down once they are potted, but the colours are re-spotted. When all the reds have disappeared the colours are taken in rotation from the yellow and when potted stay down. With the potting of the black the game ends and the player with the highest score is the winner. If the players' scores are level at this stage, then the black is brought back into play to decide the issue. Thus there can be no question of a tie.

A red counts one point. The colours, each of which has its own spot on the table, are valued as follows: yellow (2), green (3), brown (4), blue (5), pink (6) and black (7). Penalties are incurred for going in-off—that is losing the white—and for missing or hitting the wrong ball, and these are to the value of the ball being played with a minimum of four points. Such points are added to the opponent's score. All this is simple enough, and I do not think anyone will have much difficulty in understanding it, but it is a much more difficult thing to be able to play the game well, or attain any degree of proficiency. In fact, to become really proficient takes the best part of a lifetime.

For example, all the present-day professional players started playing the game at the age of eight, nine or ten, and it is only after years and years of practice and experience that they have become experts. In my opinion a player does not reach his peak until he is at least forty-five years of age.

Joe Davis, the founder of the modern game, and the greatest player the world has ever seen, played his finest snooker between the ages of fifty and fifty-four. His delayed peak was probably due in some measure to the war when there was a lull in competitive play.

It is fair to say that the average snooker-player in this country is of novice standard. The percentage of people who advance from that standard and get higher up the tree is very small. Just look at the size of the entry for the Amateur Championships. This is perhaps about four hundred. Yet there must be well over four million players in the country. Obviously there are reasons for this. Perhaps the main one is that so very few people ever start the game in the right way.

In this respect I was fortunate, for you might almost say I was brought up on a billiards table. My father, who was a very good amateur player, opened a billiards hall at Plymouth when I was six years old. Three years later he took over a billiards club at Exeter and it was there at the age of nine that I first started to knock the balls around. I used to drag a mineral case around the table to stand on because I was not tall enough to reach a full-sized table. My father gave me early tips and coaching. In other words I was put on the right lines from the start. Under his guidance I was able to make my first billiards century at the age of twelve and a half. After experience in the Boys' Billiards Championship, where I lost by one point to Barrie Smith—later to become the professional John Barrie—I turned to snooker and in 1946 entered and won the Amateur Championship. At twenty-two years of age I was the youngest-ever champion. I decided to become a professional, but so wide is the gap between the amateur and professional that

I had to undergo an intensive training period of five years, practising eight hours every day before beginning to approach the top flight of the game which culminated in my winning the World Professional Match Play Championship in 1958, the last time it was played.

This was effectively the World Professional Snooker Championship since all the leading professionals competed in it although it lacked the sanction of the Billiards Association and Control Council, who were then the governing body of both the professional and amateur games.

The political rift was temporarily healed in 1964 when I beat Fred Davis for the title, successfully defending it seven times until 1969, ten years a sworld no. 1. My only regret about this period is that it was before the current Snooker boom, which increased the potential earning power of every professional in the country. I must confess that even when I was no. 1 it was often difficult to make ends meet.

Nevertheless, the essence of any true professional player lies in the fact that he loves the game he plays so that at no time did I think of shelving it in favour of something which might have been a little more remunerative. This may be a cynical age but I am quite certain that no one will ever approach the top of any sport unless he has this genuine love of the game. Only in this way could he put in those necessary arduous hours of practice which are essential for success, hours which I spent in a billiards room entirely on my own, finding out something about the game. Although I was Amateur Champion—and as such a good player—I really knew very little about the finer points of the game.

I studied and practised hard until the time came when, whether I played a shot and got it or missed it, I knew the reason. This enabled me to make certain of correcting my mistakes. It is just not good enough to miss a shot and dismiss the fact with a shrug of the shoulders. You must know why. This is the secret of consistency, one of the big differences between the amateur and the professional.

Perhaps this little preamble into my own beginnings will help to explain why there are so few really expert snooker-players. It needs many hours of concentrated practice and an apprenticeship far longer than that of most other careers.

First and foremost you must start on the right lines if you want to make progress. Unless you are taught correctly from the beginning your game will be sloppy and restricted. You will develop bad faults which will be hard to eliminate later. You must learn to stand properly; to hold the cue correctly; to make a firm bridge and develop a correct, smooth cue action. In this book I shall attempt to guide you along the right path, but I do not by any means claim that I am going to turn you into a top-class player. The written word can never do that. However, if you study what I have to say I am sure you will be able to assimilate sufficient knowledge to improve your game.

It will be of no use just skipping through the pages at one reading and then thinking you know it all. Read it again so that the important points will become more firmly embedded in your mind. Then go through the book chapter by chapter, making a careful study as you compare your own style. I do stress that you pay particular attention to those chapters on the stance, bridge and cue action. These subjects are the basic fundamentals. If you conquer them you will be well on the way to proficiency.

I

Stance

Many people, on taking up snooker, cannot understand why they make so little progress at the game. Slow development can nearly always be traced to faulty style. In other words they have not learned the A B C of the game: correct stance, bridge and cue action. It is the result of a haphazard introduction to the game.

The majority have their first experience of playing the game when they are persuaded to join in with some friends. A cue is stuck into their hands and they are told simply to 'knock the balls into the pockets'.

They find the cue hard to manipulate, but by watching others they attempt to play. Unfortunately, it is seldom that there is anyone present to tell them how the cue should be held and managed, and how they should stand. So Mister Average Player is to all intents self-taught. He develops his own style, and probably does all the wrong things.

For the want of better knowledge he pursues his original style. But his faults are a great handicap, and soon get so ingrained that they become practically impossible to eradicate. They prevent him from becoming a good player and thus gaining greater enjoyment from his game.

Unless you stand correctly, and deliver the stroke correctly, you will never progress at the game, no matter how many hours you practise.

There can be no half-measures—learn the fundamentals

of a good stance from the start. Don't just pick up the cue and hit the balls anyhow. You will only regret it later.

Though it is far better to have the practical first-hand advice of a coach who can show you exactly what you are doing wrongly, I shall try to steer you along a path which, if followed closely, should help you to improve.

So let us start with the A B C of snooker. First I shall deal with the stance. Obviously, the short man will stand at the table differently from the tall man, but the basic principles apply to both. Flexibility is the key, and this can only be achieved by perfect balance.

The easiest way of explaining this is that the stance for snooker is similar to that for boxing. The same principles apply. Weight must be evenly distributed and the body perfectly poised so that there is no movement on the stroke apart from that of the striking arm. Place your feet as if you were going to fight. They should be comfortably apart, the exact distance depending, of course, on your height. Then bend forward, getting your chin well down to the cue.

You will notice, if you do this correctly, that your front leg is slightly bent, while the rear leg is straight, acting as a bracer. Weight is evenly distributed, but if anything slightly forward on to the front leg.

The forward leg, although bent, must not sag at the knee, otherwise this could lead to a swaying movement. Make sure that the rear leg is ramrod straight, the foot slightly turned outwards but kept firmly on the floor.

Point the body in the direction in which the stroke is being made. Plate I brings these points out in my own stance.

The whole essence of this position is to make you perfectly balanced and at the same time comfortable, and that is how you should be if you follow these directions carefully. You have learned your first lesson.

Common faults are: rising on the toes of the back foot; spreading the legs sideways; holding the legs too far apart, or too close; and bending both knees.

So examine your stance carefully and make sure you eliminate these faults. Practise until you are satisfied that you are getting down correctly, for, believe me, this will enable you to play better and therefore gain more enjoyment from your game.

2

The Bridge and Holding the Cue

Next we consider the bridge, the channel through which you guide the cue to make contact with the ball.

This is a comparatively simple thing, yet many players make a poor bridge. They overlook its importance, being content just to place the hand on the table. Too often it is weak and inclined to move. And remember that first lesson of the stance: only the cue arm must move, the rest of the body should remain perfectly still.

First, place the left hand (right hand in the case of a left-hander) flat on the bed of the table, spreading the fingers approximately one inch apart. Now draw the knuckles up until their highest point is about two inches from the bed of the table. Keep the fingers taut, gripping the cloth with the fingers and the heel of the hand. Now cock the thumb until the first joint makes contact with the forefinger. This should provide a nice 'V' along which your cue may travel (see Plate 2).

I cannot overemphasize the importance of the grip on the cloth. It should be so tight that should you lift any finger with the other hand, when released it would immediately snap back into position on the cloth.

The bridge must be quite immovable, and the accuracy of your shots will depend on just how well it has been made.

The left arm should be extended as straight as possible without creating any strain. Some people are inclined to bend the left arm a little, but this has the effect of bringing the bridge too close and making everything cramped. So I repeat, stretch the arm as far as possible without tension, your bridge hand gripping the cloth but with no strain. You should feel comfortable.

Let me now deal with the holding of the cue. Firstly, the grip. This has always been a controversial subject, and even among good players you will find variation. Some prefer to hold the cue lightly, just gripping the butt with the tips of the fingers; others want to hold it tightly. My own experience is that the cue should be held firmly. I recommend that you take the cue in the palm of the hand, wrapping the fingers around it. It should be held firmly, but it must not be *gripped*, because this sets up tension in the arm, a tightness which would restrict the movement.

So hold the cue firmly, but loosely enough so that it could easily be pulled out of your hand.

The cue must always be held in the palm of the hand. If you were going to knock a nail into the wall you would not hold the hammer in your finger-tips, for this would give you no control over it. So it is with holding the cue (see Plate 3).

There is also the question of *where* to hold the cue. I always hold it right at the end, but this depends largely on the particular balance of the cue and the physical make-up of the player. A short man, for example, may well find that he is better able to balance the cue by holding it three or four inches from the end.

It must be held so that it is comfortably balanced in the general line up of the stance, and this will vary slightly with different cues. Whereas one cue may need to be held right at the end, another may balance if held further along. This is something that can only be determined when you get your particular cue in the hand. The thing I want to stress is that you must be comfortable, with the cue perfectly balanced.

The cue can now be placed on the bridge between thumb and forefinger with the tip protruding about six inches. Provided you have followed these instructions closely your cue should now be under perfect control while travelling freely over the bridge.

There should now be a direct line through your bridge to

the right shoulder, with the right arm hanging perpendicularly over the cue. The elbow must not be cocked in, or out. This should then leave the cue arm to swing freely, and independently, from the elbow without affecting the rigidity of the upper arm and shoulder (see Plate 4).

This is such a vital position that it is advisable to get a friend continually to check that your forearm is perpendicular and not leaning slightly to the left or right.

Your position can also be checked by cueing in front of a mirror.

Plates 5, 6 and 7 show my cue action at three stages of a normal follow-through stroke. Plate 5 shows the cue-tip initially addressing the cue ball. Plate 6 shows the cue drawn back prior to making the stroke and Plate 7 shows the cue at the full extent of its follow-through.

3

Cue Action and Sighting

You are now ready for the swing, or cue action. This is effected by the movement of the forearm only. The shoulder must be kept perfectly still, with the forearm swinging to and fro like a pendulum. Provided you carry out this movement correctly, the cue should travel backwards and forwards with a piston-like action, which should be short and compact.

The cue should not travel more than four to six inches, but this, of course, will vary slightly according to the type of stroke being made. The wrist must be supple so that the cue always moves parallel with the bed of the table.

One of the most common faults of cue-swing is to make the movement from the shoulder. This must be avoided at all times. The movement must be made only from the elbow, with the cue travelling parallel to the bed of the table. The stroke should be delivered cleanly and smoothly.

All this may sound simple in print, and I have no doubt you are wondering when you will be ready to hit the ball! But I cannot stress enough how important the initial groundwork is to your future development.

In fact, it is well worth spending a few weeks doing nothing else but practising swinging the cue so that it becomes instinctively correct.

This, of course, applies to all sports where an implement designed to strike the ball is used. The implement—in this case the cue—must become virtually an extension of your right arm. Without this affinity between the snooker player and his cue he cannot become even a mediocre player, let alone a match-winner.

Although most of you will have no pretensions of becoming champion players, you must want to get somewhere . . . if only to become good enough to beat your friends. And the satisfaction of beating someone you consider a better player than yourself will only come if you are prepared to give thought to the smallest details.

Now let us turn to sighting. People have different ideas of how this should be done. Some never bother to get their heads down at all, but this inevitably means a loss of accuracy.

The chin should be down on the cue so that you can look right along it. You would not think of firing a rifle when holding it at your waist; you would hold it at eye-level. Exactly the same thing must apply to the cue. You have to get your head right down so that you can sight along it. The closer you can get to the line of fire, the more accurate your shot is likely to be.

Here I must make special reference to the head. Like the legs, this can control body movement, so it is essential that you keep it still while making the stroke. Get into the habit of staying down on the stroke, at least until the cue ball strikes the object ball.

I cannot emphasize enough that all movement must be eliminated except for the action of the cue arm.

It is a good idea at first to keep the head down until all the balls have come to rest. This will help to eliminate that common fault of jerking up the head at moment of impact.

Now to the actual sighting of the balls. I have made a pretty close study of this, having carefully watched my brother professionals, and I have reached the conclusion that there can be no hard-and-fast rules about it. Experts all seem to tackle it in a slightly different way, except for one important fact that is common to all of us: whatever motions the eyes have gone through while addressing the cue ball, at the moment that the cue tip strikes the white your eyes must be focussed on the point of contact you desire to make on the object ball.

My own method is first of all to look at the cue ball to see that the cue tip is addressing it correctly. My eyes then flick up to the object ball to see that my cue is aiming at the precise point that I desire. Then I go through the same process again to make sure that nothing has moved. As my eyes come back to the object ball I go through with the stroke.

While this sighting is taking place, the cue is, of course travelling backwards and forwards with a short piston-like action, and my mind and muscles are getting set to deliver the stroke at the required pace. As my eyes flick back to the object ball for the second time, the cue has just started its forward motion. And if my eyes tell me that everything is in order I go right through with the stroke. The golden rule, as in golf, is 'Keep your head down'.

4

Striking the Ball

So far we have dealt with the A B C, the stance, the bridge and cue action, and provided you have digested these instructions you should be ready to face up to the ball in the right manner. I can sense you saying: 'Ah, at last we are going to hit the ball.' But I must impress upon you that snooker is not a game to be hurried. You have to walk before you can run. Any attempt to skip these fundamentals can only lead to sloppy play later and subsequent disappointment when things do not go right.

So here we are ready to hit the first ball . . . but you are not ready for making big breaks yet. There is still a lot more to learn.

Our next step is to concentrate on striking the cue ball correctly.

The essence of all shots in snooker is to be able to strike the cue ball at dead centre. That is not as simple as it may sound. There is so little margin for error that consistent potting can only be achieved by striking the ball in the right spot. A little deviation to one side or the other and the ball will not run true.

It is not merely good enough to guess at what spot you think is the centre. You only learn this by trial and error and the exercise for this is continually to play the ball up and down the table.

Place the cue ball on the brown spot and play it over the blue, pink and black spots to the top cushion. Those spots are the guiding line.

The object is to get the ball to rebound off the top cushion and run back over those same spots until it returns to the tip of the cue.

Sounds simple, doesn't it? But try it and see. You will find it much more difficult than you think.

You will not have much trouble in playing up over the spots. It is the return journey that proves the difficulty. It will probably come back wide to the left or to the right of the cue. This is because you have not hit the cue ball exactly in the centre. You have struck it to the left or right, according to which way it returns. In other words you have applied side, that is side-spin, which takes exaggerated effect when it comes off the cushion.

A ball that is spinning cannot run true, and at this stage you must concern yourself only with plain ball striking. In fact, play the majority of shots plain ball. The question of side is more advanced, and I will deal with it later. So at this stage forget all about side, except to avoid applying it.

To return to that 'up-and-down-the-table' stroke, this is your first lesson in striking the cue ball. And until you can do this accurately you will never make any headway.

You must practise and practise this stroke. With reasonable care you will be finding the central spot to strike about once in five attempts. Then you may take heart. You will be starting to learn. Later you will find it more consistently.

Don't overlook or skimp this practice. I know it can be boring. But even professionals are continually practising it. They must be certain of striking the ball correctly before they move on to other stages of their own practice. And remember that professionals are always practising. It is the only way that they can keep at the top of their form. What is good for the professional must be good for you.

Take my tip—every time you go to the table, play a few of those up-and-down-the-middle-of-the-table strokes to get your eye in. And do that even when you have gained a certain amount of proficiency. I repeat, you cannot practise it enough.

Clean and accurate striking of the cue ball is the key to successful potting.

Before leaving this chapter, which aims to help you get a good cue action, there is one other point that I must mention—the cue ball must always be struck with the tip of the cue, and not pushed.

In the old days of billiards the stroke was more of a push because the technique of that game demanded a more gentle, flowing type of action. All three balls had to be controlled and they could only be coaxed into position with delicate play. Snooker, however, is a much more forceful game. Here only the cue ball has to be controlled, as the object ball, of course, finishes up in a pocket. One's only concern, then, is the satisfactory positioning of the cue ball for the next stroke, and the modern technique of the game has been developed so that this is achieved more often than not by the use of stun and screw. This, as I have said, tends to make the action much more forceful.

I point this out at this stage so that you may develop a definite punch into your striking of the cue ball. This will pay dividends when you become more advanced.

Remember, however, that the stroke must still be cleanly delivered, and the cue must follow through except when playing the stun stroke. This is the only stroke at snooker where the cue must be stopped suddenly on impact with the cue ball. But more of that later. At this stage it is enough to concentrate on achieving an aggressive type of cue action with a good follow-through, remembering at all times that your body and head must be kept perfectly still on the stroke.

5

Potting

To 'pot' is to strike the object ball with the cue ball and knock it into a pocket. This is obviously much more difficult than controlling just the one ball, which we discussed in the previous chapter. With two balls there is a double margin of error. Unless you strike the cue ball accurately you cannot expect to make the precise contact on the object ball.

The part of an object ball that has to be struck in order to pot it is the point of the ball that is furthest away from the pocket. To find this, draw an imaginary line from the centre of the pocket through the middle of the object ball and where that line emerges is the desired point of contact.

For a better understanding of this look at the accompanying diagram (Fig. 1). You will see the pocket and one red ball, with a number of cue balls scattered around to cover all strokes possible to pot the red into the pocket.

No matter which cue ball is used, the point of contact on the red to knock it into the pocket is the same. I have marked it with a cross.

It is a question of finding the right angle, but if you remember the point furthest away from the pocket you cannot go wrong.

Having got this clearly in your mind the next problem is to play any of the cue balls into the desired position. This is best achieved by imagining a ball already at the point of contact (as per diagram). In order to aid your sighting of the shot it is a good idea actually to place a ball into the position of the imaginary one (in the diagram). Then get down as if to play your shot, carefully noting the area of the red covered by the 'imaginary' ball.

When you have determined this, take away the intervening, or imaginary, ball, and play your shot confidently, being careful to remember the previous exercise and to strike the cue ball centrally.

This last point should emphasize how important it is to master the fundamentals of the game, for until you have perfected hitting a cue ball centrally you will not be able to strike the red ball in this exercise at the correct point, no matter how you try.

Once again, practise this continually. Don't skimp it. Keep on at it until you become consistently accurate.

Having studied the theory of potting you should now be ready to put this knowledge into practice with some simple pots.

Obviously, the easiest pot of all should be the one which is perfectly straight. Here you will be sighting along a straight line of the cue, the cue ball, the object ball and the pocket.

However, there is one thing to remember. The greater the distance between the cue ball and the object ball, and between the object ball and the pocket, the more difficult the shot is. Obviously, this is because of the distance the balls have to travel.

Most people, when they have been playing a while, can knock in the reasonably easy pot when the cue ball is not too far away from the object ball. But they find this becomes increasingly difficult as the distance increases. Greater accuracy is needed. When the balls are close you can sometimes get away with a slight discrepancy. But the greater the distance, the more any slight error is magnified. A clean cue action is what enables the player to produce the necessary accuracy. I must once again lay stress on stance and cue action, the fundamentals of the game, so get those perfected at the start.

Now for a few easy pots when the balls are close. Place

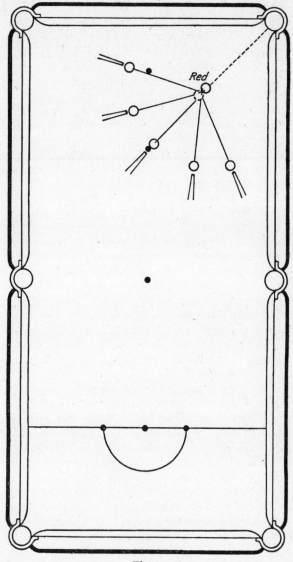

Red

Fig. 1

the balls in the position shown in Fig, 2. Check over the instructions I have given so far. See that the stance is right, feet comfortably apart with weight evenly distributed, and get your chin down on the cue. Check your bridge to see that it is rigid; see that your cue arm is hanging perpendicularly and hold the cue firmly, but not tightly.

Make a few preliminary waggles with the cue to see that you have the right action and that you are sighting correctly along the line. Then play your shot.

Don't try to force the ball through the back of the pocket. Just hit it with a nice even stroke, striking the ball and following through smoothly with the cue.

Probably you will not make the pocket at the first attempt, and this may be because you were not sighting the ball properly.

Here, then, let us return once more to the question of sighting.

I suggest you follow this procedure. First look at the centre point on the cue ball, and line up your cue to be certain that you are aiming at the correct point of contact and that your cue is travelling in a horizontal line. Then, as the cue begins to move, focus your eyes on the point of contact on the object ball. Forget all about the pocket. Just concentrate on the stroke at hand and get a perfect picture of it in your mind.

To illustrate this point, I sometimes play a shot like this from memory. In fact, a gimmick of mine in exhibitions is to play a shot of this kind whilst deliberately looking the other way. First I get down to the shot and line up my aim. Then, when I am perfectly satisfied that my aim is correct, I look away at someone in the audience and fire away.

Spectators think I must be something of a miracle man. But you can perform this trick, too, if you have followed the A B C of snooker, and if your aim is right. It is merely a question of good cue action.

Now let us get back to those first few simple pots. Each time you try them, make a thorough check that you are doing everything correctly and soon you will be able to pot

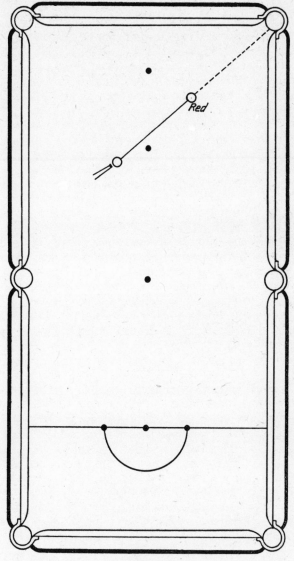

Fig. 2

the ball with consistency and accuracy. Once this is achieved, try widening the distance between the balls.

First increase the distance between the cue ball and the object ball and the pocket. Practise away at these shots, for it is only practice that leads to perfection. Never be hesitant on your shot. This can only mean that you are not concentrating properly on the stroke.

Another variant from potting over greater distances is the speed at which you play the stroke. You will find it much more difficult to be accurate when playing a shot at speed, since this can so easily produce faults in your cue action. That is why it is so essential that the cue action should not exceed four to six inches. Bear in mind that with powerful strokes it is the forward thrust of the cue which counts, not the back-swing.

Keep the cue action short and compact at all times, for it is solely this forward thrust, or 'follow-through', which determines the power of the stroke.

A very important point to remember here is that even with the maximum follow-through at the end of the stroke the cue must still remain parallel with the bed of the table.

In other words, the tip of the cue should follow the path of the cue ball.

Before you attempt anything else be absolutely certain that you have mastered the technique of stance, sighting and cue action for the straight pot, and that when making the straight pot the object ball goes cleanly into the pocket . . . ten times out of ten. When you can do that you are getting somewhere and will be ready to tackle the angle shots.

So far we have dealt with the straight pot only, but, of course, you don't always find the balls in a straight line when you become involved in a game. Mostly, in fact, you will have to strike the object ball at an angle. Remember, though, as I pointed out in dealing with the theory of potting, that the point of contact is always that which is furthest away from the pocket.

So let us go back to the diagram (Fig. 1) in which I placed

one red on the table and a series of cue balls. The angle is different each time. I have often been asked: 'How do you work out the right angle?' The only answer is: though you may have little idea at the start, it will come with practice and is really a question of estimation. Get down to the shot, and look at it first this way, then that, until you are certain that you are right. Remember here the aid of the 'imaginary' ball.

The diagram shows the limits of the angle from which a ball may be potted into a particular pocket.

First try the pot from position 'A', which is slightly off straight. Then, as you gain proficiency, move on to the further positions marked 'B', 'C', 'D' and so on.

If you find you are failing to pot the ball consistently you must look to your sighting and cue action for the remedy. First, however, note on which side of the pocket you are missing. It is possible that it is on the same side each time, which indicates you are sighting incorrectly. So make a slight adjustment to the angle and try again.

One of the big differences between the professional and the amateur player is that when a professional makes a mistake he registers why, and sees that he doesn't repeat it. This is something you must learn to do.

Once you have found that you can pot the ball with reasonable consistency from the first simple angle, look for further variations, as in the previous exercise, by playing the stroke at varying speeds, then by lengthening the distance between the cue ball and the object ball. Obviously, the greater the distance the more difficult the shot, as the further the cue ball has to travel before making contact with the object ball, the greater the margin for error.

You'll find with the very short-range pot that the ball may still be potted via the corner of the pocket, even though a slight misjudgement has been made. With the long-range pot, however, the error will become so magnified that the pocket can be missed by several inches.

6

Getting Into the Game

So far you have had a lot of theory to absorb and a number of shots to practise. You are no doubt anxious to try all this out in an actual game. Well, provided you have mastered all these techniques, you should be able to pot a ball fairly consistently, and be ready to turn theory into practice. So, try a game.

It doesn't matter with whom you play, your pals at the local club will do fine. And don't worry about the result, it is of no importance at this stage. All I want you to do now is implement all the points I have made, and to get an idea of the game in action.

Remember to check back repeatedly on points of technique, position of the cue and so on. In fact, it might be a good idea occasionally to give yourself a spot-check during the game. Ensure that your stance is right, that your bridge is firm and rigid and that your cue action is short and compact. In other words, thoroughly aquaint yourself with the proper procedure for every move you make.

Treat this period of your tuition, if you wish, as a 'breather' from arduous practice. Practice may not only be arduous but monotonous: I know this only too well. In the twenty-eight years since I turned professional, after winning the Amateur Championship of 1946, I have spent hours and hours at practice.

I still find it necessary to practise every day, and so does every other professional.

Between 1946 and 1951, a period of five years, and quite

the stickiest part of my career, I spent eight hours a day in a billiards room, entirely on my own. It was a period of intensive training when I was finding out about the game. For although as the Amateur Champion I was already a good player, there was a wide gap to bridge to reach professional standard. I found that I didn't really know why this happened, or why that happened. And that is what I had to learn in those five arduous years.

I don't expect you to spend that amount of time at practising. Unless you are completely dedicated it would only make you sick of the game. But you must do a certain amount simply to gain any reasonable proficiency.

It is useless to force anyone, or for anyone to force themselves to practise any particular game for a specific time. That I feel is quite the wrong approach. Practice will only do you good if you are really getting stuck into it 100 per cent and are really concentrating on what you are doing. These are the only times that practice is of real value. If you are forcing yourself when you don't really feel like it, it will do more harm than good.

It is far better to break off from practice when you start to get a little tired, and to do something entirely different.

Think of practice as gaining experience so that the cue action becomes mechanical; so that the whole A B C of snooker becomes as natural to you as breathing. It is rather like driving a car. Once you have learned the mechanics of it—shifting gears, clutching, braking, steering—what you need before these operations become instinctive is actual driving experience on the road.

And so it is with snooker. Once the fundamentals are ingrained, you are ready to learn something about the positioning of the cue ball. But that is jumping the gun slightly. Before I tell you about positioning there is still a lot of groundwork to be covered.

7

Other Types of Bridges
and Use of the Rest

Having played your first games as a breather from the study
of theory, you will have quickly discovered that the cue ball
is not always in position to make an easy stroke, and that
the basic bridge, which we dealt with earlier, is often
impossible to use. This occurs when the ball is either on
the cushion or close to it; when the cue ball is close to
another ball; and also when it is beyond your normal
reach.

To deal with these positions we have other types of
bridges. We also have the rest. First let us deal with the
other bridges, and we will start with the cue ball which is up
against the cushion (see Plate 8). This is always a most
awkward shot to play.

First see that your cue is chalked, to avoid the possibility
of a miscue. Now place the fingers flat on the edge of the
rail and drop the wrist, cocking the thumb to the knuckle
of the forefinger to make the guiding channel for the cue.
Keep your fingers flat. In this way they can grip the surface
of the cushion and form a rigid bridge. Remember, as I
mentioned in the earlier instruction on the normal bridge,
the whole essence is that the bridge must be firm, and not
sloppy in any way.

Most ordinary players try to balance the bridge on the
tips of their fingers, and at the same time raise the cue
because of having a restricted area of the ball to strike.

The stance – side view

The Bridge

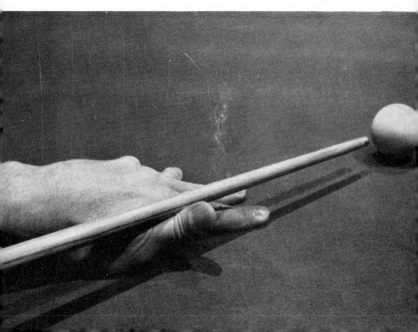

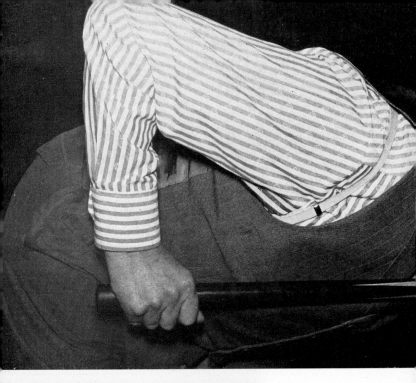

The grip and the vertical forearm

The stance – back view

Believe me, that can only lead to a wobbly bridge, and a loss of accuracy. So keep those fingers flat. And although there is not a great deal of the ball to hit, your cue action should be confident.

Don't try to force the shot or play it at speed. And shorten that cue action. The tip of the cue should just brush the cushion before making contact.

Consider next the ball that is just a few inches out from the cushion. Don't try the normal bridge; this brings you too close. Make use of the cushion and rail, with what is termed the loop bridge.

Place the heel of your hand on the rail, and the finger-tips on the cushion (as shown in Plate 9). Instead of cocking the thumb up the side of the forefinger, keep it straight and tuck it under it until touches the centre joint of the middle finger. Now loop the forefinger over the outside of the cue.

Running the cue along the cushion, let it brush the outside of the middle finger and the inside of the forefinger. This is the guiding channel. But don't allow those fingers to grip the cue or impair its movement in any way. You must keep the cue horizontal, and once you overcome the feeling that the cue is out of control you can play your shot at almost any speed required.

At first glance, the position in Plate 7 may look identical to that in Plate 6 but in fact the cue ball is a little nearer the cushion. This necessitates bringing the bridge hand further back so that only the fingers are resting on the cushion rail. From this position, I utilize the normal bridge where the cue travels once again over the V of the thumb and forefinger.

Now we come to bridging over a ball, which is one of the most awkward shots in snooker. For this you have to raise the heel of the hand off the bed of the table and rely on your fingers alone for strength and firmness. No one likes playing this shot, but it has to be played. Plate 11 illustrates this better than my words. Note particularly how the two middle fingers are forward and the other two back.

C

Spread the fingers and use pressure to see that they are gripping the cloth. Keep the arm straight. The position of the thumb is similar to that for the normal bridge, except that this time it has to be a little higher, and the stroke has to be made with a downward thrust. Don't hurry the stroke, which should be moderately paced, and don't stab at the ball. Play *into* the ball.

The height of the bridge will depend entirely on the closeness of the ball you have to play over. But the higher you have to make it, the more difficult it becomes, because it may mean that the tips of the forefinger and little finger also have to come off the table as you bring the wrist forward to get the height.

Always take your time in finding the right position for your bridge. Also, be certain that you do not touch another ball either in putting the hand on the table or taking it away. This is a foul, and will be penalized.

There are also a great number of shots for which you cannot make your own bridge. This is because of the distance the cue ball is away from the cushion. For these we have to turn to outside instruments, known as 'rests'.

There are two types—the normal rest, which has a metal cross to form the bridge, and the 'spider', which is specially designed for playing over a ball, like the high bridge made with the hand.

The half-butt and full-butt, to enable you to reach those extra long-distance shots, are in fact extensions of the normal rest which I shall deal with first.

No one likes using the rest, for it tends to break that personal control, but it is a necessary evil, so learn how to place it on the table and how to use it correctly (see Plate 12).

Far too many players tend to balance the head of the rest on the table and hold the butt in the air. This is all wrong. You must place the rest firmly on the table and hold it there. Get the head of the rest properly positioned, preferably about six to eight inches away from the cue ball, although this, of course, depends entirely on the lie of the other balls. Never place the rest too far away. The greater distance the tip of the cue has to travel, the more likely you are to err. The cue will tend to waggle, just as it will if you have the bridge made with the hand too far away.

Having found the position in which to place the rest, lay the handle flat on the table and hold it there with the left hand so that there can be no movement. This is most important.

The other important thing is the holding of the cue. This calls for an action entirely different from that used in normal play. The cue is held with the first two fingers on top of the cue and the thumb underneath. The remaining two fingers just rest lightly underneath. They don't come into the grip at all. The hand is turned away, so that the back of it faces towards the chin. As with normal play, the action is all from the elbow, only this time it is with a sideways movement.

You can sight along the cue in a direct line, and you should make the few preliminary waggles to see that you are striking in the right direction, and that the cue is moving directly forward, not to one side. Once again, don't stab at the shot. Follow through just as if you were playing normally.

You can play almost any stroke with the rest, but my advice is: don't be over-ambitious. Make it as simple as possible. Above all, be comfortable and don't try to over-reach.

The action is, of course, similar with the half-butt and full-butt.

The length of the cue on the latter rests adds to the awkwardness. They tend to waver, not having the stability of the normal cue. So don't try to play the shots hard, or fast. Be content just to play at a medium pace without trying anything fancy, otherwise you will be inviting trouble.

The action for using the spider is similar to that for the other rests, except that in this case you have to play down into the ball. Be ultra-careful with your placing of the spider. Don't try to position it merely by holding the handle and leaving the unbalanced head wavering in the air. If you do you are almost certain to foul one of the balls you are trying to avoid. Use both hands to place the spider in position. Better be safe than sorry afterwards.

Once you have the spider in position, then hold it firmly. It is not always possible to put the handle on the table, as with the ordinary rest, but you can still hold it firmly. There is always a tendency to brush the top of the cue ball when using this ungainly instrument. This will more often than not lead to a miscue, which may well open the game up for your opponent. So play down into the ball, and play it safe, being content to go for the simple pot, or position you require.

8

Stun and Screw Shots

All the potting that I have dealt with so far has concerned plain ball shots. I have deliberately avoided reference to stun and screw because you have to learn this game by easy stages. Forgive me for stressing the point again, but you cannot hurry, or assimilate everything at once. It will be no good just skipping through this book. Go through it in stages, and master each lesson point by point before moving on.

However, by now you should have achieved some reasonable control over the plain ball shot and be able to make your pots with some consistency. They will help you to make small breaks. But to make any appreciable advancement you have to learn positional play.

A 'break' at snooker is a series of consecutive pots, and to achieve this the cue ball has to be deliberately steered into position for each successive shot, so that the pots are made as simple as possible. If the cue ball is allowed to run around the table, leaving it to chance where it comes to rest, the player will soon be faced with difficult or impossible positions.

However, before you can master this phase of the game there are two essential strokes to be learned, the 'stun' and the 'screw'. These form the basis of all break-building and about seventy per cent of all strokes played will necessitate their use.

You must therefore regard the 'stun' and 'screw' as your 'bread-and-butter' strokes. Believe me, they are going to be of incalculable value to you.

The stun shot is used to stop the cue ball dead. It is used mainly on perfectly straight pots when it is desired to leave the cue ball in the position previously occupied by the object ball.

Many good snooker-players find this difficult to master. In fact it is a difficult stroke to teach, let alone execute. It is a stroke which the player himself must get the 'feel' of, by trial and error. But once you do get the feel of it, it becomes quite easy to bring off. Approach it in the right attitude, and show no hesitancy in its execution.

It is played by striking the cue ball a little lower than centre, and on the moment of impact of the tip of the cue on the cue ball the cue must stop 'dead'.

It is the only stroke in snooker which requires no follow-through.

Thus you see there are two points of difference between this stroke and the plain ball shots we have dealt with previously. With the latter you aim at the centre and follow through: with the stun, you aim low and have no follow-through.

If, when you play the shot, the cue ball still runs on a little after striking the object ball, one of two things is wrong: either you are not striking the cue ball low enough, or you are failing to stop the cue dead. Should the cue ball come back slightly after striking the object ball then you are striking it too low; or, again, you are failing to stop the cue dead at that precise moment of impact.

So you see why I say that it is a stroke of trial and error, the exact 'feel' being learned only by experience.

There are limits to this stroke. If the distance between the cue ball and object ball is too great then it is impossible for anyone but the expert to bring it off.

It is mainly used when the balls are from a few inches to three or four feet apart. The more proficient the cueist, the greater the distance at which he can perform the shot.

There are, of course, slight variations of stun, for there are times when you might require the cue ball to run through just a little. This is governed by the point of contact on the cue ball, and by the cue action. But more of that at a later stage.

It is most important for this type of shot to see that your cue is chalked. Then it will cling to the ball and set up reverse spin. So, before ever you attempt a stun or screw shot, see that you chalk the cue first—but don't *over-chalk* it. A good tip is essential, but that, and the treatment of the cue tip, will be the subject of another chapter.

Having learned the rudiments of the 'stun', it is time to turn to the 'screw' shots. These are probably more widely used than any other strokes, and it is essential to master them. Screw can be used to pull the cue ball back for position, or to take it off, at an angle other than the natural one after plain-ball contact.

There are usually so many balls on the table, particularly in the top half, that it is impossible to gain a desired position with a plain ball stroke because of cannoning into one of them. Every ball in fact becomes an obstacle which has to be avoided. This is where the screw shot comes in, for it can make positional play easier by enabling the player to thread the cue ball through the gaps.

It is played in much the same way as the stun, except that for the screw you must follow through with the cue. Many quite good players find this difficult simply because they fail to let the cue go through. Remember this as you face up for the shot, and always play it confidently.

Some players apparently have the impression that pulling the cue back quickly after impact helps to draw the cue ball back after it strikes the object ball. This is quite wrong, and must be avoided at all costs.

The screw stroke properly executed imparts a backward spin, and the amount of run-back will be governed by the amount of power and follow-through you put into the stroke.

The majority of players tend to hit the ball too high. You must strike it as low as possible, and to help in this adjust your bridge. Drop the thumb of the bridge hand, and lower the butt of the cue slightly so that the cue is closer to the bed of the table.

But be sure the travel of your cue is horizontal. Otherwise you can get a lifting action which will cause the cue ball to jump. It is probably the fear of this, or perhaps of digging into the cloth, that causes so many players to hit high on screw shots and fail to impart the necessary backwards 'twist'.

If I explain to you exactly what happens to the cue ball when a screw stroke is played perhaps it will help you in your approach to the shot. A ball that is propelled by a normal follow-through stroke starts to roll immediately after the initial impact of the tip on the ball. As it rolls, like any moving body, it produces an energy of forward motion. When it strikes a stationary ball it momentarily suffers a shock from the collision. Its own volition then reasserts itself and the ball carries on along its deflected path.

With the ball that is played with deep screw applied, however, the ball does not roll with this forward motion, it skids to the object ball, for it is in fact resisting its forward propulsion so that when it strikes the stationary object ball the collision now helps it to assert its desire to spin backwards.

The screw is another 'trial-and-error' stroke. By repeated practice you will gradually get the feel of it. The essential thing is to remember to follow through. When the cue ball and the object ball are close together it is sometimes difficult to get the cue out of the way of the returning ball. So for practice purposes it is a good idea to make this stroke with the balls slightly off-straight.

The action for both screw and stun should be short and sharp. But don't snatch at the shot. It must be smooth, just as it is in all other shots. This is where that good stance and cue action I have been drumming into you is so important. It enables your cue to move like a well-oiled piston.

I have already mentioned that the achievement of perfection with stun and screw shots is a matter of feel. You have to feel the tip of the cue bite into the ball, and you can only learn the strength of this by practice.

I have therefore worked out some diagrams of practice

shots which should enable you to get the hang of things (see Fig. 3).

In stroke 1 you will see the cue ball, a red and the black; the latter being positioned on its spot, and the red conveniently placed in potting position. This set-up illustrates the practical use of the stun shot.

You will notice that the red is a dead-straight pot into the right-hand top pocket; so if you can pot this and leave the cue ball in the position occupied by the red, it will leave you in position for potting the black.

Remember carefully my earlier instructions about the stun. Get yourself comfortable, see that your stance is right, and make sure your cue is chalked. Now choose the spot to strike on the cue ball, remember just a little lower than centre; take a short back-swing and aim. At the moment of contact stop the cue dead.

Provided you have carried out everything correctly the cue ball should send the red into the pocket and stop in its place, in perfect position for potting the black.

There is no better way of getting on the black. You are, of course, having to divide your concentration between potting the red and the positioning of the cue ball, so at first you may find you are missing the pocket. Don't worry, just try it again and again, making slight adjustments each time until you succeed. Remember it is a question of trial and error to find the right action. When you find it make a mental note of exactly what you have done. Then keep repeating the stroke until it becomes automatic.

I cannot emphasize enough that this can only be conquered by practice and not luck. You will never get anywhere on luck alone.

Stroke 2 is a simple practice shot for the application of screw. In the diagram you will see that the red ball is placed on the blue spot, with the cue ball directly behind to give a straight pot into the centre pocket. The object here is to pot the red and at the same time screw the cue ball so that it comes straight back into the opposite middle pocket.

Obviously this shot would be undesirable in a match, for

it would mean giving points away to your opponent. As we all know, the art of snooker is to keep the white on the table and never let it go into the pocket. Nevertheless, this is a very useful stroke for practice purposes only. If you are worried about the cue ball coming back on to your cue, make the shot a little off straight and be content to bring the cue ball back to the cushion. You'll find this exercise a test of cue action to indicate whether you are striking correctly.

Now let us return to the application of screw, to ensure that you are performing it in the correct manner. First make your check: stance, cue action, bridge. Remember that this time you must follow through, and allow the tip of the cue really to bite into the cue ball. Don't forget the lowered bridge, and that the cue must run parallel to the table and not downwards.

After having gained some proficiency with bringing the ball back into the pocket, forget this shot completely, and practice elsewhere on the table. Place a colour in a position to the rear of the cue ball. Now play the screw until you can get the cue ball to come to rest in the right spot for getting on the colour. Try this from various angles and shorten or lengthen the distance. Only in this way will you be able to judge the strength needed to bring the ball back at varying distances.

Remember, though, that the deep screw is impossible when the cue ball is too far away from the object ball. For the amount of rotation that you apply to the cue ball decreases the further it has to run to the object ball.

Stun and screw shots need a lot of practice, so don't despair. If a shot is worth learning it is worth learning well. You will gain your enjoyment later when your breaks start to increase. There is nothing like the satisfaction of break-building. It gives a warm feeling of something achieved.

I have often heard ordinary club players say, after just knocking the balls: 'I just cannot understand it. I can never pot more than two or three balls in a break. They just don't run for me.' No wonder, I think. It is because they have not

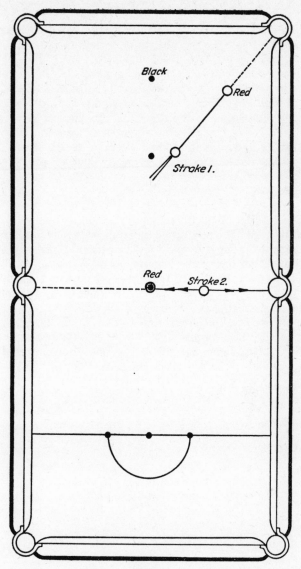

Fig. 3

made sufficient study of the game to make the balls 'behave'. They rely too much on chance for where the cue ball is going to stop.

Only by cue-ball control can you make successive shots simple, and even the simplest shot can be missed. More times than not this is due to carelessness, and not paying sufficient attention to the fundamentals. The player says: 'Oh, this is easy' and forgets all about bracing himself on the stance and pays insufficient attention to the stroke at hand. The resulting position of the cue ball has always to be considered with even the easiest of pots. So never be careless.

Always keep your eyes open for the stun and screw to obtain position. And treat every stroke on its merits. You probably have to concentrate more in snooker than in any other game. That is if you want to master it, rather than have it master you.

Finally, look back once again over the intricacies of stun and screw and try to pin-point your faults. Too little spin because the ball has not been struck low enough? . . . dipping cue? . . . no follow-through? . . . snatching? . . . weak bridge? . . . sloppy stance?

Avoid these faults like the plague, and always be ready to check and re-check that you are doing the right thing.

9

Positioning Around the Black

Having added two more vital strokes to your repertoire, you should now be in a position to make breaks of a reasonable size. So why not take time off from studying and try to put into practice something of what you have learned so far. Don't worry about trying to win. Use your games as practice, in which you pay every attention to detail. Provided you have assimilated the instruction so far, the breaks are bound to follow.

I don't by any means claim that, having read so far, you are ready to become a complete player. Far from it. For you cannot learn by reading alone. Theory on its own is not enough. In addition, you must have the practical experience, like an apprentice learning a trade. However, provided you have grasped the fundamentals you should find a general improvement in your game.

And here I repeat yet again: don't forget that stance and cue action. They are easily the most important skills of all in snooker, and unless you have conquered them you cannot hope to make progress.

Often a player who has a good idea of the game, and who is aiming correctly, still fails to achieve the pot. This is because his cue is not travelling on the correct line. And to get the correct movement the stance must be just right.

Once you have had your game or two it will be time to return to study. We will now move on to positional play.

The layout of the table is such that the black, the highest scoring ball, is at the top of the table. It is around this ball that most big breaks are built. As you know, scoring is done by potting a red and a colour, alternately, until all the reds are cleared. After this all the colours are taken in sequence. Remember how they count: yellow (2), green (3), brown (4), blue (5), pink (6) and black (7). Potting black completes the game.

Obviously, then, the ideal is to try to take the black with every red, then your score would add up to a maximum of 147.

As I say, that is an ideal, the pinnacle of achievement, but very few players in the whole history of snooker have ever performed such a miracle. Joe Davis, the greatest player the world has known, and the man who is really responsible for the amazingly high standard of snooker today, has only achieved it once and he has been playing snooker longer than some of us have lived. In fact, he retired as undefeated World Champion, after holding the title for twenty years, in 1946, the year I won the Amateur Championship and decided upon a professional career.

But we are getting away from the subject of this chapter, which is positioning around the black. Like top-of-the-table play in billiards this is the position to achieve and maintain for a big break. But everything depends on the lie of the reds, and sometimes you will be forced to come down the table to take other colours in order to keep the break going. Generally you must use these colours to lead up to the black-ball position. It is the one ball around which there is a close constructive game.

You can keep a break going here as long as there are sufficient reds around, but you will need an extensive repertoire of strokes, particularly the stun and screw strokes dealt with in the previous chapter. Your objective must be to make every shot as simple as possible. In Fig. 4 I give you the layout of a break of twenty-four, concentrated solely on the black-ball game.

At first sight the diagram may seem a little complicated, but follow the instructions carefully and its purpose will soon become apparent.

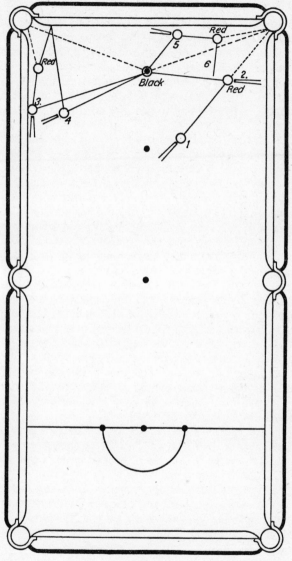

Fig. 4

There are three reds, all conveniently placed. Position 1 shows the identical stroke used for practising the stun shot, in which the red is potted into the top right-hand-corner pocket and the cue ball stunned to take the red's place. This leaves you in position to pot the black into the top left-hand pocket. Play the shot with sufficient follow-through and strength for the cue ball to run into position 3 on the side cushion.

The next red is then potted into the top left-hand-corner pocket, once again with a follow-through action so that the cue ball runs into position 4 via the top cushion, leaving you nicely on the black. This second black is then played gently into the top right-hand-corner pocket with the cue ball running into position 5 on the top cushion.

The third red is also potted into the top right-hand-corner pocket, and here we once again employ the stun stroke. By applying stun for this pot, which is slightly off-straight, you should be able to stop the ball at position 6, which leaves a nice, easy third black, for a break of twenty-four.

Incidentally, to achieve the run-through it is not necessary to put top on your cue ball. Strike just a little above centre and make sure that you follow through with the cue. It is only necessary to strike the cue ball at the top when an excessive amount of run-through is needed.

If you play this practice break exactly as I have indicated then every shot should present an easy pot. The exercise should give no trouble at all provided your cue action is correct.

Practise this break several times. But take care over each individual shot. Don't hurry. Treat every shot on its merits and make sure your cue action, backed up by a firm comfortable stance, is correct.

The stun shots should not trouble you unduly provided you take care to aim low and hold the cue at moment of impact. With the follow-through shots in this break of six shots it is a question of judgement of pace. Whatever you do, don't try to force the stroke. That can only lead to error. Work out exactly where you want the ball to stop, concen-

Addressing the cue-ball – preparing to strike

Addressing the cue-ball – the backswing

The shot itself – follow through

Bridge for playing from tight on a cushion

trate on the right amount of application; then, when you are sure this is correct, switch your concentration to potting the ball at hand. Work it all out in easy stages, but beware of an unequal division of attention, otherwise either the pot or the positional play will suffer.

10

Potting the Colours

By now you will have learned the rudiments of making a break around the black. You must always keep your eye open for this sort of set-up when you are actually involved in a game. Always look ahead to the possibilities of a break, not merely to the next colour. This, of course, comes with experience, but I know only too well that many quite good players never visualize more than one stroke ahead.

Now let us turn to the potting of the colours after the reds have gone. I don't suppose that at this stage you will be able to clear the table successfully, but it will be your ambition.

So here is a useful exercise for practising your potting and positional play. In the diagram (Fig. 5) you will see all the coloured balls (a total of twenty-seven points) on their respective spots. The cue ball placed in an ideal position for potting the yellow, which is, of course, the first ball in sequence after all the reds have gone.

Here we can have a practical demonstration in the use of screw. From position 1 the object should be to pot the yellow into the bottom right-hand-corner pocket, at the same time applying screw to the cue ball so that it returns to the position whence it started. This will put you in a nice position to pot the green, which is the next ball in order.

Now don't forget the lesson of screw. Correct stance . . . lower the bridge . . . and strike low so that the cue tip bites into the cue ball . . . and let the cue go through. This should bring the cue ball running back to the desired position.

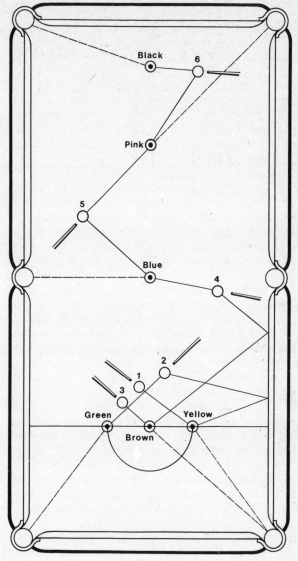

Fig. 5

The green, of course, is potted into the bottom left-hand-corner pocket. Once again, use a little screw to pull the cue ball back for position on the brown, as shown in Fig. 5.

You will probably find that the next stroke, the potting of the brown, is a little more difficult because of having to judge the strength of the cue ball over a greater distance. However, don't be afraid of it. You should have had sufficient practice now on the screw shots over a variety of distances, provided you have not been rushing through the earlier stages of this book.

The brown is potted into the bottom right-hand-corner pocket, and the cue ball given sufficient screw to make it strike the side cushion just below the middle pocket, then rebound at the natural angle into position 4. This places it nicely on the blue.

This position must be clearly noted, as it is most important that the cue ball should come to rest slightly below the line of the middle pockets. This is because you want to send the ball up the table with the next stroke.

Obviously, if the cue ball finishes above the centre line of the blue and middle pockets you are in trouble, for the only way then to the pink would be via the cushions at the bottom of the table. This would mean the ball having to travel such a distance that you would find it difficult to get 'on' the pink at all, except perhaps for a long-range shot at an awkward angle.

So concentrate on trying to obtain the position indicated. This leaves a comparatively simple shot. Just play the blue gently into the left-hand middle pocket and use sufficient follow-through action for the cue ball to run into position No. 5.

The pink now goes into the top right-hand-corner pocket, and once again it is a question of following through for the cue ball to achieve position for a comfortable pot on the black.

It all sounds so simple, doesn't it? And it can be, provided you play each shot correctly. Cue action is of vital importance, and it calls for sustained concentration. Play each shot individually, and erase from your mind all thoughts of the next shot (except, of course, your position of the cue ball) until you come to it. Concentrate on the shot in hand. Too many players break down because they let their minds run ahead too quickly.

It is seldom, of course, that you find all the colours on their spots at the end of a game, but it serves as a useful potting and positional exercise for you to try. Many a game has been won and lost on the colours.

By practising such a set-up you improve your own prospects in the event of such an opening coming along. In any case, while the colours may not be on their respective spots they may be near at hand, and with a little variation you can get into position to take the lot. This gives any player a feeling of intense satisfaction.

In the main you have to try to maintain position above the baulk colours to pot them into the bottom pockets; and to keep below the blue. In other words, you must move up the table in easy stages, always keeping the cue ball under control.

II

Breaking Off

It may seem to you that I have put the cart before the horse in dealing with positional play around the black, and the potting of the colours, before dealing with the opening stroke of a game of snooker. However, the foregoing were really practice exercises, and were mentioned for this reason and not in relation to their order or importance in the game.

In some games the initial stroke is relatively unimportant, since it merely serves to set the game in motion. But this is not so with snooker. Very often a distinct advantage can be gained from a well-played 'break off'.

After winning the toss in the professional game we never think of allowing our opponent to 'break off', and neither should you. Use the initial stroke to leave the balls safe, and make the position as difficult as possible for your opponent by trying to bring the cue ball down to the bottom end of the table. If your opponent can be tempted into making a mistake with his first stroke it may pave the way to a break.

Many games are won on an early break, for it gives the opportunity to take a vital lead. In the professional game it could start a break of fifty or sixty. The ordinary player cannot expect a break of that size from a faulty break-up of the pack, but he can often gain a useful start.

It is all part of the strategy of the game.

Often, of course, several shots are played before a red is potted, but the initiative is in the hands of the player who breaks-off.

In Fig. 6 I have shown three different methods for

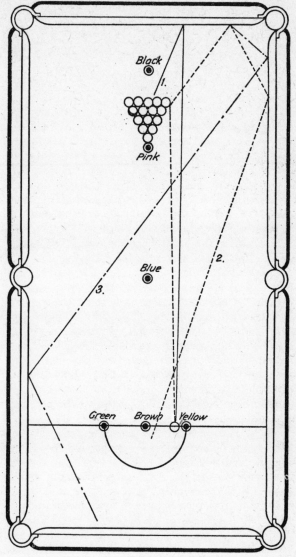

Fig. 6

starting the game and I will deal with each in turn. In each case place your cue ball between the yellow and the brown.

For No. 1 the cue ball is played on to the top cushion with left-hand side, so that it rebounds into the top of the pack with just sufficient strength to make contact with the reds.

This stroke has the obvious advantage of keeping the pack intact, leaving no possible scoring stroke for your opponent. Yet I have never favoured this. It is a somewhat negative stroke, almost as though you were afraid to make the opening gambit. Moreover, it leaves a very simple safety stroke for the next player, who may even effect a snooker behind the black, via the side and top cushions. You are certainly not making things difficult for him, and that is what your objective should be.

No. 2 shows the most common 'break-off' used by amateurs. The object here is to bring the cue ball back to the baulk cushion via the top and side cushions, after contact with the corner red of the pack.

This is a very sound method, as the pack will not be greatly disturbed and the cue ball is left as far as possible from the reds. The one drawback with this stroke is that all too frequently the cue ball 'kisses' into the yellow or brown on its way back down the table, leaving one's opponent with an easily accessible cue ball, instead of being awkwardly placed on the baulk cushion.

Now turn to No. 3, which I shall call the professional stroke. Although the objective is still to bring the cue ball back to the baulk end of the table, the path the cue ball takes is vastly different. This is because the shot is played with right-hand side applied to the cue ball. Side causes the ball to come off the top cushion higher up the table and sending it across the table above the blue, and on to the opposite side cushion. From there it again rebounds to the baulk cushion. This avoids all possibility of kissing the baulk colours. Further, the opponent is left with a most awkward shot from the cushion and the possibility of being snookered behind the green.

Sometimes the professional will aim at the end red of the second row, still using that running side to alter the angle of throw. Use of this depends on just how much you want to disturb the pack.

And that in turn depends on your proficiency and how you feel about the strength of the opposition. If you feel your opponent is not over-strong when playing from this distance, and that by having broken the pack a little wider you have a better chance of an early break, then try the end red of the second row, by all means.

Remember, however, that distance is again the big handicap. The target is small, calling for absolute accuracy in cueing. There is also the risk of brushing the end red of the third row which may send your cue ball into the top right-hand pocket and cost you four penalty points. In fact, this is what happens with many ordinary players when they attempt this 'break off'. It is mainly due to inaccurate sighting, which becomes magnified over the distance, or failure to strike the cue ball in the correct spot.

Because of this risk I would recommend that you go for the corner red of the triangle. It is better to be safe than sorry. In any case you will still leave your opponent tied up provided you have played correctly. And remember that every time you leave the cue ball on the baulk cushion you still have the initiative. Always aim to leave the other chap with the awkward shots.

You must fence for the opening to get in with a break. So don't rush. Keep that initiative!

12

The Nap of the Cloth and its Effect

I think I must break off at this point to discuss the bed cloth on which the game is played. This plays a very important part in the running of the balls, so some understanding of it is essential.

You will have noticed that the cloth has a definite pile on it, like that on a carpet or a piece of velvet. This is known as the 'nap', and is responsible for the marks the fingers of your bridge hand make.

The nap always runs the same way—from the baulk end to the spot end. *Up* the table is *with* the nap; *down* the table is *against* the nap.

It has a definite and consistent effect on the travel of the ball, for which allowance must be made.

To put it in an easy way, the nap of the cloth only makes a difference to any real extent when playing down or across the table. When playing towards the baulk you are playing against the nap of the cloth, and the tendency is for the ball always to be pulled towards the side cushions. To explain it more practically, if you are potting the pink from its spot into the centre pocket at a reasonable pace you must always play it not into the middle of the pocket but towards the bottom bump. By the time it arrives, the nap will have pulled it, so that it will enter the pocket itself.

Similarly, when playing a ball to the bottom pocket from the top of the table you must aim at the bottom cushion jaw, for the nap tends to pull the ball towards the side cushion.

This, of course, applies mainly when playing the ball

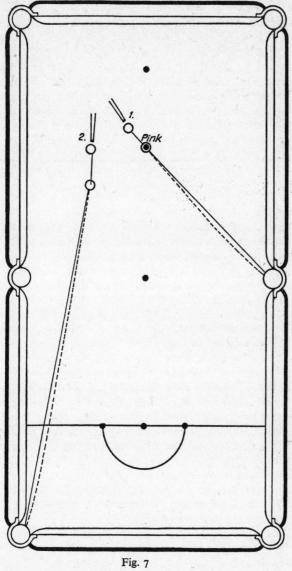

Fig. 7

reasonably slowly. If you are playing the ball hard then obviously it is travelling so quickly that the nap does not have time to take effect.

In playing across the table the pull is towards the top cushion. For instance, when playing the blue from its spot into the middle pocket the ball will tend to drift towards the top bump. The deviation is, of course, slight, but can make all the difference between successfully potting the ball or missing it. Perhaps this explains why you have missed so many of those slow pots in the past? Next time make due allowance by aiming at the bottom bump, then the pull will guide it into the pocket.

Fig. 7 gives some examples which explain what I have written. In stroke 1 you will see the pink on its spot with the cue ball nicely placed as I have already explained. The dotted line from the pink shows the path to the pocket, so aim just slightly to the left to allow for the pull.

I must emphasize that the nap does not present a problem when the stroke is played firmly, since the extra speed of the ball resists its pull.

Stroke 2 shows exactly the same effect on the long pot into the bottom corner pocket, again only when the shot has been played slowly.

Many of you will have noticed that you are far more successful with the slow pot along the top cushion than you are with the identical shot along the baulk cushion. Again this is entirely due to the effect of the nap. With the pot along the top cushion the nap is constantly pulling the ball towards the cushion, thereby helping to keep it in position. At the bottom end of the table quite the reverse applies. Here the nap is pulling the ball away from the cushion, which in turn is, of course, away from the pocket.

A few practice shots will enable you to judge the pull of the nap, which varies from table to table, according to the newness of the cloth.

Many a good table has been condemned as out of true merely because of ignorance of the effect of the nap on the slow-running ball.

13

Safety Tactics

One of the objects of snooker should always be to make the position of your opponent as difficult as possible, so in this chapter I am going to deal with safety play.

This is a phase of the game that is of more concern to the better-class player. The novice has really very little need to bother himself with safety tactics, for on the one hand his opponent is unlikely to be of sufficient prowess to warrant making the game more difficult for him, while on the other his own ability is such that he will be unable to take full advantage of any resulting 'leave'.

However, the further one progresses up the ladder, the more important safety tactics become, until at the professional level a sound knowledge of this part of the game is as essential as break-building.

Apart from the obvious occasions, when there is no possible scoring stroke on, there are no set rules about when to play safe. This must always be decided by the player concerned. Only experience will teach him when to chance the difficult pot and when to play safe.

Many things will help him to decide: the state of the score, how many balls are left on the table; and, not least, his own frame of mind at the time. A player faced with a certain position may, because he is 'on form' and seeing the ball well, elect to go for a difficult pot, whereas if he has not got his eye in, and so lacks confidence, he will prefer to play safe.

You must always see that the risk is justified. If the

difficult shot is likely to lead to a break it may be worth chancing. But if the resulting leave is likely to be awkward then a safety stroke is clearly indicated.

Some players find a great fascination in laying snookers. With a smirk on their face they will say: 'Now try to get out of that one.' Of course, it produces a sense of achievement, just as it does when you successfully get out of a particularly nasty snooker. But don't overdo this phase. It is often a sign that you lack confidence in your own potting ability. Moreover, if you try to concentrate too much on snookering it can have an adverse effect when you do start going for the pots. It is far better to mix potting and safety play. But, as I said before, when to use safety play depends largely on the state of the game, and that you will learn by experience. So be certain that it is going to pay dividends. Don't just play safe for the sake of it.

I much prefer to see an attacking game of snooker, with safety play only being used to make openings. For the average player safety strokes assume most importance towards the end of the game, when only a few colours are left on the table. At this stage of the game one badly played stroke can mean defeat.

Remember that safety play is not necessarily the laying of snookers. It is leaving your opponent with nothing 'on' and making things really difficult for him. To illustrate this, Fig. 8 shows a diagram of a couple of strokes when only the pink and black remain on the table.

Stroke 1 shows a position with the black on its spot and pink on the left side cushion. The best safety shot here is to hit the pink full in the face with a very firm stroke, driving it around the table, as shown, to the baulk cushion.

Stroke 2 shows another awkward position on the pink, which is also on the left side cushion. This time the pink is played on to the left side cushion so that it rebounds to the opposite cushion. From there it travels to the baulk cushion while the cue ball travels back to the top of the table. Both these strokes may result in a snooker, but in any case the pink will be perfectly safe.

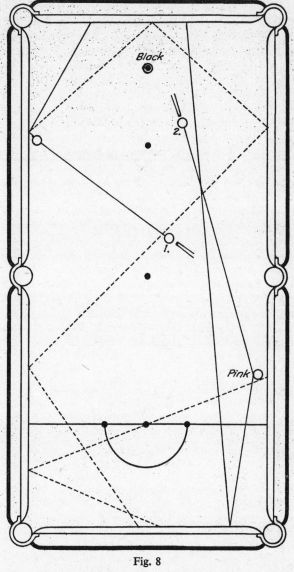

Fig. 8

There are other occasions, usually at the beginning of the game, where perhaps only one or two reds have become dislodged from the pack and a difficult pot may be attempted with a modicum of safety in mind. This usually takes the form of a long-range pot into one of the top corner pockets following a safety stroke by your opponent. With this type of shot it would be foolhardy to attempt a slow pot in order to stay at the top of the table for the pink or black. Far better in these cases to play the stroke at sufficient speed to ensure that the cue ball will come down the table to the line of the baulk colours. In the event of potting the red you will be nicely on one of the lesser colours. On the other hand, if the red is missed a fair degree of safety is ensured by reason of having brought the cue ball well down the table. These are often termed 'shots to nothing'.

Make no mistake, for the good player a sound knowledge of safety tactics is most important. He must always be trying to force his opponent into making the mistakes that will create his openings. He must always try to retain the initiative. Continually leaving your opponent in a difficult position will have a great psychological effect on his confidence, and will gradually undermine his morale.

Every player will plan his tactics differently, according to his particular temperament. My advice is to be bold without ever being reckless.

14

Snookers

The laying of snookers, it must be acknowledged, plays a very important part in the tactics of the game. From the beginning to the end of a frame one must always be on the look-out for a snooker that is likely to pay dividends. By this I mean that very often the well-thought-out snooker may be of greater benefit than an attempt to pot.

Take, for example, the position shown in Fig. 9. The player has potted a red and has left the cue ball in a reasonable position for potting the brown into the middle pocket. This may well be accomplished, but it would be practically impossible to send the cue ball to the top of the table for the remaining reds in order to keep the break going. Here, then, is the obvious occasion for laying a snooker behind the brown. From this position any player would do well to hit a red, but the important point is that he would be practically certain of leaving a favourable position, whether he in fact made contact with a red or not.

This to my mind typifies the main use of the snooker. It is to force one's opponent into a position where, in endeavouring to hit the ball 'on', he is likely to leave a favourable position for a break.

We all know that snookers often become vital at the end of a game, when only the colours remain, and when one needs to make the opponent forfeit points if one is going to have any chance of winning. A player may be thirty points behind, needing a forfeiture of at least four points and all the colours to win.

67

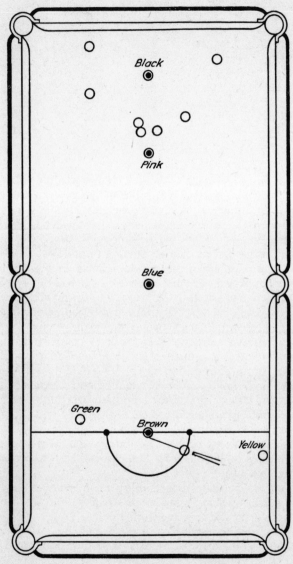

Fig. 9

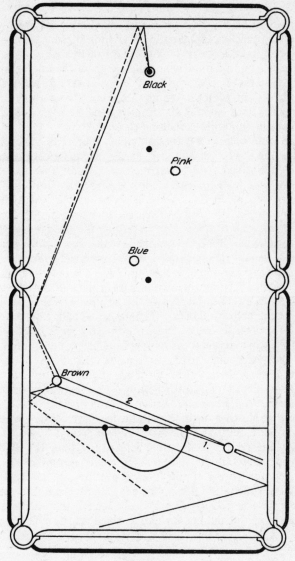

Fig. 10

It would be pointless for me to spend a lot of time here in attempting to explain the thousands of snookers that may be played from various positions of the balls.

Every game of snooker is different from the one before. There are no set positions, so one has always to make the best of the situation that applies. However, there are certain principles that should be strictly adhered to, so I will content myself with explaining these.

On these occasions it is essential at all times to be certain of leaving the object ball safe. Never play a snooker which sends the object ball towards a pocket, for the obvious reason that in the event of not getting your snooker the colour will be left on. Generally speaking it is usually advisable to play the cue ball behind an obstructing ball, as the closer one can get the cue ball to the obstruction the more difficult will be the snooker. At this stage of the game one is usually hampered by one's opponent, who, if he knows the game at all, will be dribbling his pots so that in the event of missing them he will leave the ball close to the pocket. One is then faced with the position of either having to pot the ball, so reducing the number of balls that can be used for obstruction, or endeavouring to keep it out of the pocket, which in most cases makes the playing of a snooker on that particular stroke extremely difficult. A lot will depend upon the position of the next colour. If this should be conveniently placed for getting a snooker it may well be advisable to pot the ball that is over the pocket.

Fig. 10 shows a position with the last four colours left on the table. It illustrates the advantage of getting the cue ball nicely behind an obstructing ball, rather than the object ball. As you will see, the resulting snooker from stroke A is a comparatively simple one to circumvent via the top cushion, with a little side on the cue ball. Stroke B, however, when the cue ball is played nicely behind the black, is a much more difficult proposition. It will need to be played off at least two cushions, which, of course, calls for extreme accuracy.

In many cases there will be alternative ways of playing a

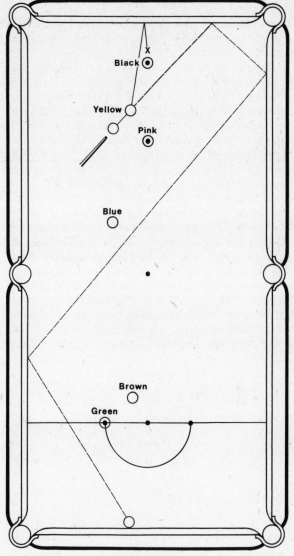

Fig. II

snooker. Naturally, one should always endeavour to play the one that will result in the most difficult position for the opponent.

To illustrate this point look at Fig. 11. This also emphasizes the inadvisability of ever playing a snooker while driving the object ball towards a pocket. At first sight the obvious stroke to play appears to be a gentle one on to the yellow, sending it towards the top right pocket whilst nestling the cue ball behind the black. An error of judgement, however, must inevitably result in the yellow being left over the pocket. Even if the stroke were successful the resulting snooker would not be too difficult.

In my opinion the stroke shown in the diagram is much the better one. Here the yellow is played firmly on to the top cushion so that it rebounds around the cushions to a position at the baulk end of the table. The cue ball is stunned so that it goes on to the top cushion and back behind the black. The resulting snooker is now extremely difficult to negotiate. And, in the event of failing to get behind the black, the yellow will be perfectly safe.

A good knowledge of angles is essential, and this is why the good billiards player will often shine at this particular phase of the game. Laying snookers is practically the same as playing cannons.

15

Getting Out of Snookers

I have dealt with the laying of snookers, so now let us look at ways and means of circumventing them. After all, snookering is not all one way. You have to know how to get out of them, as well as how to lay them.

Escaping snookers is generally a matter of knowing the angles. Some, of course, are real teasers, leaving the position completely hopeless. In such cases I must leave you to your own devices. However, there is usually some way out by using the cushions. It may mean using more than one cushion, so you have to calculate the different angles at which the ball could rebound.

As the knowledge of angles is the first essential, I suggest you try this simple exercise. Drive the cue ball hard from the brown spot on the baulk line to a spot on the top right-hand cushion, about a foot from the pocket, and make a mental note of the angles it takes. See that you hit it 'plain ball', then it should run to true angles. Make variations of this shot from different points. Then try it again with the application of side, to see how that alters the angles. This, of course, is all experiment with no other balls on the table, but it can teach you a lot and is well worth spending some time at.

The single cushion 'get-out' should not provide undue difficulty when the distance is not too great, but it is surprising how many ordinary players fail. This may be because they are not aiming at the correct angle, or because they are inadvertently using side. Remember that when playing off a cushion it is essential to strike the ball as correctly as when potting a ball.

How do you find the correct angle? Well, I suggest that you stand away from the table, examine the position and look to the point of the cushion which would make a perfect 'V' between the cue ball and the object ball. It may well be that the cue ball and object ball are not in a direct line, so that one side of the 'V' is shorter than the other. In cases like this draw an imaginary line through the shorter leg until it does level up. That will give you your true angle. Having decided this, you can then move in and play your shot.

Another method of playing out of a snooker, which is often overlooked by the average player, is by making use of the jaws of the pocket. By playing on to one side of the jaw the ball will rebound on to the other, then go off along the cushion at almost a right-angle. Similarly, it is also possible to use the jaw of the middle pocket—though in this case you use only the one jaw to deflect the ball to the desired degree. Don't use side, and don't play too hard or this can cause the ball to jump.

Go for the shot boldly and don't be afraid of going in-off; the pockets are too tight for that, provided you hit the centre of the pocket jaw. Just remember the number of times you have missed a pot because your ball has 'boggled' in the jaws and you will see you have little to fear. There is always a comfortable sense of achievement in bringing off this shot, and in most cases it will leave a look of amazement on your opponent's face. It is not a trick shot, just plain use of the angles.

The average player is usually content just to get out of a snooker, and will often merely take a bang at the ball more in hope than good judgement. That is the wrong approach. At all times you should attempt to control the ball and look ahead to see what is likely to happen if you do successfully contact the object ball. Sometimes there is more than one way out of a snooker. Don't merely take the path which looks the easiest; work out which is the most advantageous. You have to try to leave everything safe, for, as I have mentioned before, snookers are not necessarily laid for the penalty points they may gain but for the position they leave afterwards. Many a big break has started from the results of a successfully laid snooker.

a. A single-cushion escape. Note the V shape made by the cue ball leaving the cushion at the same angle at which it struck it.

b. A three-cushion escape using the natural angles. Never use side unless you have to.

c. An escape using the pocket jaws—the only way in this instance.

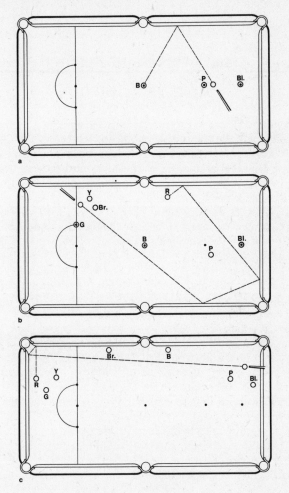

16

The Swerve and Potting
Along the Cushion

Everything I have written so far puts the emphasis on a cue action where the cue travels parallel to the bed of the table. Now I am going to deal with a shot where this does not apply. It is the swerve, a stroke which most players would like to master, as it gives a great deal of personal satisfaction in its achievement.

If you want to be a useful player this is a shot you must learn. It can be a most effective reply to a snooker, for instead of sending the ball in a straight line it causes it to describe an arc.

Most players tend to think that such a shot is beyond their capabilities, and so avoid it like the plague. Yet it is not as difficult as it would appear, and with a little practice you will soon find that you are able to use it with considerable efficiency.

As I mentioned at the start of this chapter, this time you depart from the horizontal path of the cue. You raise the butt of the cue to an angle of around forty-five degrees so that the tip strikes down into the ball, either to the left or right side according to which way you want the ball to swerve (see Plate 13).

The big difficulty here for most players is the raising of the butt. It means a higher bridge and you attain this by lifting the heel of the hand off the bed of the table. Thus the whole bridge is supported on the finger-tips. The tendency is for a wobbly and uncertain bridge, but press firmly with the fingers. The tips of the middle two fingers remain in the same position as if making a normal bridge, but the fore and little fingers move slightly back and therefore give extra support.

The amount of swerve you place on the ball depends on how high you raise the butt. If you raise it almost vertically the amount of spin applied can be so great that it will cause the ball to complete a semicircle. This is the 'Masse' stroke, more widely used in billiards, but, of course, it can also be useful in snooker.

However, we are dealing with the swerve. Strike the ball downwards with a firm stroke. Feel the tip bite into the ball. The effect of this is to push the ball out until the spin takes its grip on the cloth, which then pulls it back into line.

You must have a reasonable distance between the cue ball and the intervening ball, and between that ball and the object ball, to use this stroke effectively. You will see such a position in the accompanying diagram, Fig. 12, where swerve has helped to get out of a nasty snooker.

In this position you will see that the last red is snookered by the blue. In fact every other colour is guarding the approach to the red via the cushions. It is an obvious occasion to use the swerve. Strike the cue ball on the left-hand side and aim at a point just to the right of the blue. This sends the cue ball out to the right, and when the left side spin starts to work it pulls the ball back on course to make contact with the red.

With lots of practice considerable accuracy can be achieved with this stroke, and it can be used even to the extent of potting a ball.

A shot that most players hate is the pot along a cushion. You will all have faced a situation when a red is resting against a cushion, and, although it is only a foot or so from the pocket, the tendency is to express doubt at being able to pot the ball.

Of course, it is difficult to pull off because the ball must

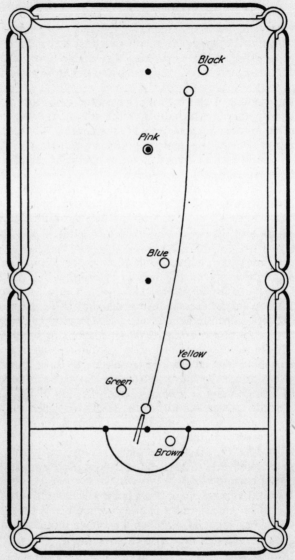

Fig. 12

travel directly along the cushion to the pocket, which from this angle appears only half its normal size.

There is only one way to pot this ball. The cue ball must strike both the red and the cushion simultaneously. This, and only this, will cause the red to roll along the cushion to the pocket.

If the red is struck slightly before the cushion it will bounce off and so miss the pocket. Similarly, if you strike the cushion first then you do not make the correct contact on the red. So your target must be to hit both the red and the cushion together.

Some players find that they achieve more success with this shot at the spot end of the table than they do along the baulk-end cushions. This is due entirely to the effect of the nap. Remember we dealt with nap of the cloth in a previous chapter, and here is where it can take effect. When playing the stroke at the top end of the table the nap will naturally tend to pull the ball towards the top cushion. It is therefore helpful in keeping it on course.

The reverse applies when you are playing at the baulk end of the table, for you are playing across the nap and the ball is pulled away from the cushion and therefore away from the pocket. So, whenever you are faced with this shot at the baulk end of the table, it is advisable to play the stroke a little more firmly so that you give the object ball less time in which to run off.

After seeing these cushion shots played with apparent ease, in professional matches I have often heard spectators remark: 'How do they do it? I can never play that shot successfully.'

It is merely a question of knowing what to do, and then approaching the shot with confidence. Practise it for a while and you will soon learn to sight the stroke correctly and begin to pot it with some consistency. Above all, don't play it tentatively. Like all strokes at snooker, it needs the utmost confidence.

17

Black Complex

At this stage let me pin-point a common fault among average club players. It is the tendency to have a go at the higher-valued colours regardless of the difficulties involved in making the shot. And this happens more often than not with the black.

The player becomes so obsessed with the fact that he can score seven points with one stroke that he is oblivious to the existence of the other colours.

This is what we call a 'Black Complex', and it should be avoided. You must bear in mind that big things often have small beginnings, and this is particularly true of snooker.

After all, what is the good of taking seven from one shot and having your break end there? Had you gone for the yellow, or green, which had better positional prospects, you may well have gone on to take several more balls to build a reasonably sized break.

First and foremost when potting a red you must endeavour to get on a colour . . . and in most instances it should be the easiest colour, not necessarily the one of highest value. You must always make your shots as simple as possible. That, of course, is the secret of the professional's success. He can bring off many spectacular moves, but it would only be a matter of time before he broke down if his every stroke were an ambitious one.

So forget about being black-conscious; go for the shot which serves you best from a positional value. Only in this

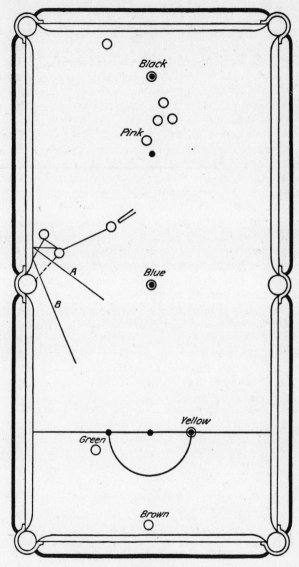

Fig. 13

way can you expect consistently to compile worthwhile breaks.

By all means try to get position around the black. That is the easiest position to work in because of the close proximity of the reds. But use the other colours to get there by easy stages rather than take a risky shot to get at once to the top of the table.

Plan your breaks ahead from the lie of the table. There will be occasions when, due to circumstances such as an unforeseen kiss, you will not be so favourably placed even though you have potted the red. When this happens you must scrap the preconceived plan, reappraise the situation and make another plan to suit the new position.

In Fig. 13 you see an example of this. The position shows all the colours on their spots with several reds in the top half of the table, one in particular being nicely 'on' for a pot into the middle pocket. The player decides to pot this red with left side on the cue ball so that it will spin off the cushion for position on the blue (see line A). Having played the shot, he finds that although he has potted the red, the cue ball has kissed into the red on the cushion, causing it to spin off down the table (see line B). From this position the player would be unwise still to play the blue; far better to pot the yellow into the corner pocket, and screw the cue ball up the table via the side cushion on the remaining reds.

One bridge for use when the cue-ball is near a cushion

And another!

Bridging over a ball

18

Avoiding the Obvious In-off

Snooker is full of pitfalls. How many times have you played a scoring shot only to find that your cue ball has gone into a pocket as well so that instead of scoring you have given away a penalty? There are many traps like this, and a little study of where your cue ball will finish after you have played your shot will show you when they are on.

There is nothing more heartbreaking than to go in-off when a game is 'all on the black'. We have all seen players pot the black, only to lose the white through not paying sufficient attention to where the cue ball might finish.

I can give you a classic example of this that occurred when I was playing an exhibition at a club. Normally I give starts to club players, but on this occasion the local champion wanted to play me on level terms. He got away very well, and maintained the initiative with some clever safety play which had me struggling.

In fact I had my back to the wall until eventually I managed to get in and square the game. Now all depended on the black. I breathed a little more freely, but misjudged a pot and left an absolute sitter into the top right-hand pocket. This was it. I was going to suffer the ignominy of a defeat at the hands of a club player, for it needed only a gentle shot to pot the black.

But the local champion, his pals cheering him on, became over-confident. He wanted to finish in a blaze of glory by crashing the black home. It went into the pocket all right. There was no mistaking the accuracy of his potting. But because of that crashing shot the cue ball flew twice round the table and disappeared into the middle pocket. So it was game to me and my prestige was saved, and all because the local champion had forgotten to look ahead. He learned a hard lesson that day, and I am willing to bet that he was much more wary the next time he was faced with a similar situation. So my advice to you all is to learn from this experience and remember always to watch for traps.

Shots which would be a delight at billiards are quite the opposite in snooker. They occur because the ball follows a natural angle into a pocket which the player has not bothered to check. In fact, when you don't want them those pockets can be just like a magnet.

So make a mental note whenever you get trapped in this way, and see that you avoid it next time.

To help you with this I have made a series of diagrams in Fig. 14 to show some of the most common 'in-offs'. They usually occur when playing half-ball shots. Sometimes you can see the danger there but must still go for your pot. In such cases you should use a little side or screw to pull the cue ball away and avoid the natural angle.

One of the most common of these traps is where the blue is positioned on its spot in the centre of the table and is potted into the middle pocket from a point just below the opposite middle pocket. Played without stun or screw, this is a natural angle into the top corner pocket. Obviously your method of avoiding this disaster must depend entirely upon the position which you desire for your next stroke. That is to say, the average player will be content to merely pot the blue and apply just enough screw or stun to avoid the in-off. But the player who thinks ahead in the game will not only get the pot and avoid the in-off but will also manage to position the cue ball correctly for his next stroke.

The point I have just made is probably the most significant of anything you have learned so far. No player, however diligently he practises, can ever hope to be more than a mediocre player unless he can think and plan ahead while playing. It is not good enough, if you wish to be a champion,

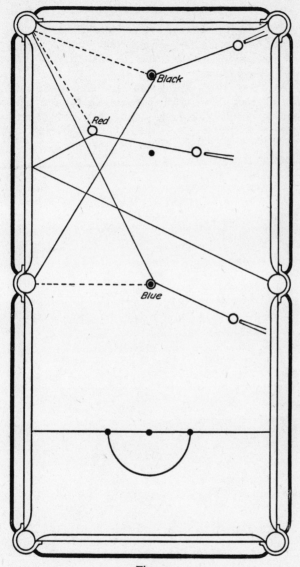

Fig. 14

to get the pot regardless of everything else. For you might find that, as a result of your erstwhile points-scoring pot, you have badly positioned the cue ball so that you are unable to score further.

The diagram (Fig. 14) shows a half-ball pot into the top left-hand pocket, which often results in the cue ball rebounding off the side cushion into the opposite middle pocket.

The Plant, and Use of Side

I am going to deal with a stroke of which little or no use is made by the average player. It is called the 'plant', and is a stroke in which the cue ball is played on to a red which, in turn, knocks another red into a pocket. This sounds extremely complicated but in fact is not as difficult as one would imagine. With a little practice I feel sure that the average player can make much more satisfactory use of the stroke than at present.

Always look at the lie of the balls and see whether a possible 'plant' is there. The easiest and most obvious of 'plants' is, of course, when two reds are touching each other and are in direct line to a pocket. You no doubt know that if you play as if to pot the first red the second will travel directly into the pocket. This I have illustrated in the diagram (Fig. 15) and it is so elementary that it needs no further explanation. However, the ball must be hit properly and it is as well to play it at a reasonable speed so that the nap of the cloth will not cause it to run off.

Now let us look at stroke 2. This is where you make your own plant, when two balls are an inch or so apart and not absolutely in line with the pocket. It means that the first red must be played on to the second red at the correct angle if the second red is to be potted. How, then, to judge this angle?

The best way of determining this is to look along the line of the two reds, imagining that the first red is the cue ball. You must determine the line along which the first red must

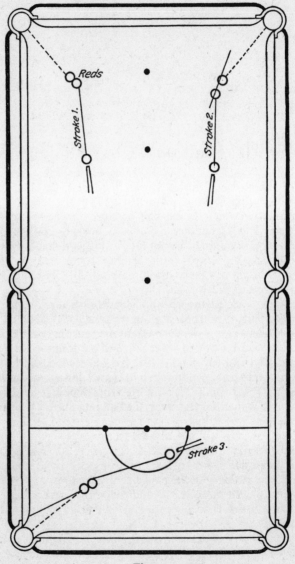

Fig. 15

travel in order to pot the second, as I have shown by the line in the diagram. Having got this firmly fixed in your mind, play the cue ball on to the first red so that it travels along the line, and the second red will be potted. It calls for accurate striking of the first ball, but once you begin to get the idea of this you will be surprised at the number of times you'll make a successful stroke.

Stroke 3 is different again, and it seems to defy logic. In the diagram there are two reds touching each other, and not in line with the pocket. They are in line with a point on the side cushion, some two or three inches from the pocket.

You would think to have any chance of making this plant that the first red would have to be struck on the left-hand side, in much the same way as stroke 2. In fact, this is not so, because the two balls are touching and remember this only applies when they are. From the position shown, if the cue ball is played on to the right of the first red the second red will deflect towards the pocket. It does not seem to make sense, but try it for yourself and see.

When two balls are touching, the second ball can only be sent along the direct line of the plant if the first ball has been contacted as if to send it along that line. If the first ball is struck to one side or the other of this point a squeeze takes place which causes the second ball to deviate from the line of the plant. This then is what we have used to make the plant which doesn't appear to be on.

A little experimenting will soon give you an idea of what may or may not be achieved with this type of shot. In view of what we have learned, never treat the obvious touching-ball plant carelessly. It can still be missed if the first ball is inaccurately struck.

So far I have deliberately avoided more than a casual reference to the use of side. 'Side' is a very complex factor of the game, and needs a great deal of study if its uses are to be fully appreciated.

You will already know what is meant by side. It is the application of either right- or left-hand spin to the cue ball, and is often used by players without their fully realizing its complications.

Let me first emphasize that side never helps you to pot a ball. In fact it always makes the pot more difficult. So the average player should restrict its use except where it is absolutely necessary.

Its main and most useful function is to cause deviations of the cue ball away from the natural path in order to gain a more favourable position for the next stroke.

Most players are under the impression that side only takes effect when the ball strikes a cushion, but this is not entirely correct, although it is, of course, then that its effect is most noticeable. Its path on the bed of the table is also affected.

You will remember in the chapter dealing with the 'swerve' how the path of the cue ball was made to curve by the application of side when striking down into the cue ball. Exactly the same thing happens with a normal stroke when side is used. The cue ball is pushed out to the right or left, according to which side is applied, and is then brought back on to the line as the spin begins to take effect. In other words it is a swerve in miniature, the curve of the cue ball being less accentuated by virtue of a normal stroke having been played instead of striking down into the cue ball. You will see from this the difficulties that arise in striking an object ball accurately when having to take into account this curving of the cue ball.

This may all sound terribly complicated but we haven't quite finished yet. The nap of the cloth has its own very definite effect on the ball that is spinning, and this effect varies according to whether the ball is travelling with, against or across the nap. When playing with the nap, that is to say up the table, the cue ball tends to pull constantly in the direction of the side applied. So a ball played with left-hand side will tend to pull to the left of the straight line, and with right-hand side will pull to the right.

When playing down the table, however—which is, of course, against the nap—you will find that quite the opposite happens. Now the ball carrying left-hand side will tend to pull towards the right, the one with right-hand side towards the left.

The amount of this swing varies considerably and will depend upon certain factors: the speed the ball is travelling, the amount of side that has been applied and also the condition of the cloth on which the stroke is played. Obviously the newer cloth will have a much heavier nap than one which is well worn, and a heavier nap will, of course, effect the ball to a far greater extent. You will realize by now that I was not overstating the case when I said at the beginning of this chapter that the use of side is very complex.

To be able to strike an object ball accurately, when all these things have to be taken into account, requires a great deal of study and practice, so that the average player would do well to restrict the use of side at first to the simpler strokes. As I have explained before, side is used in order to steer the cue ball into a more favourable position for the next stroke. But this can often be achieved with the use of stun or screw, which I consider to be far easier.

There are, of course, occasions when side has to be used, so let us now consider its possibilities. As I previously mentioned, the main use of side is to alter the path of the cue ball after it strikes the cushion. Stroke 1 in the diagram (Fig. 16) shows what happens when a ball is played on to a cushion with right- or left-hand side applied. You will notice that it comes off at an appreciable angle, instead of coming back over the same line of travel as it would with a normal plain-ball stroke

How, then, to use this fact to advantage? My next two diagrams show practical uses. Stroke 2 in Fig. 16 is a positional move. The red is nicely placed over the middle pocket with the blue on its spot (obviously the colour to get 'on'). The stroke is played with left-hand side on the cue ball, which, after it has potted the red, causes it to spin off the side cushion into position X. The advantages of playing the shot in this way are two-fold. Apart from having got nicely 'on' the blue, you have achieved a position below the

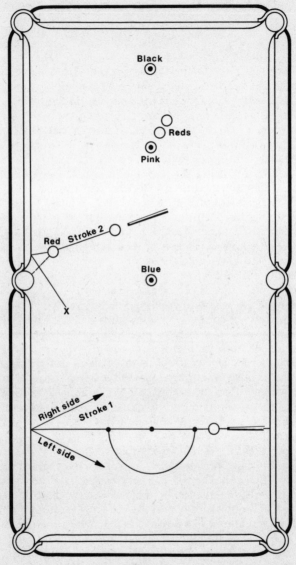

Fig. 16

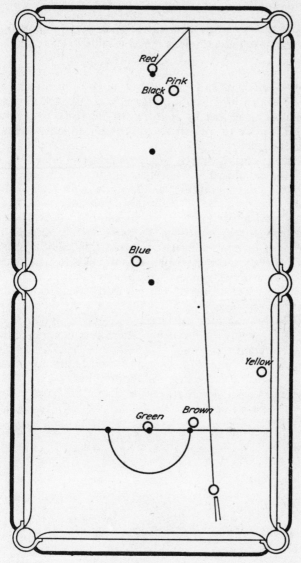

Fig. 17

line of the middle pockets which, when potting the blue is going to take the cue ball up the table towards the remaining reds.

Fig. 17 shows rather a nasty snooker; the last red being covered by the brown, pink and black. A normal stroke on to the top cushion would bring the cue ball back into the pink and black, but by applying left-hand side to the cue ball it is made to spin off the top cushion to make contact with the red.

I hope that this chapter will have given you some idea of the uses and difficulties of using side, and encourage you to devote a great deal of time and study to the subject before you attempt to use it frequently. You may well think that I have made the whole thing sound too frightening, but these strokes are so difficult, particularly at long range, that I felt I could not overestimate the difficulties involved.

Once again these are the important points to remember:

1. Don't use side unless it is absolutely necessary.
2. Study the swing of the cue ball, whether with or against the nap.
3. Make sure that you don't strike down into the cue ball, as this will inevitably cause a greater swing of the cue ball.
4. Beware the long-range shots, which are far more difficult to judge than the shorter ones.
5. The use of side is purely positional. It always makes the pot more difficult.

20

The 'Double'

The double is a stroke that the professional players use to great effect to keep a break going, but which the average player seems either to disregard completely or to approach very tentatively. Make no mistake, this is a very valuable stroke to learn. And there is no reason why even the average player cannot bring it well within his scope.

The double means playing a ball on to the cushion so that it rebounds into a pocket on the opposite side of the table. It is usually a middle pocket, although it can be played into the corner pockets as well.

The success of this stroke depends upon one's knowledge of the angle of rebound from a cushion. As this angle varies according to the speed at which the ball is played, it would be as well to spend some time merely playing a ball on to the cushion at varying speeds and noting the angle of rebound. The very hard strokes are to be avoided, as a ball played too hard on to the cushion depresses the rubber to such an extent that it is practically impossible for it to rebound at a true angle.

Now I must explain what I mean by a true angle. A ball travelling at reasonable speed will rebound at exactly the same reverse angle as it goes on. In other words, the angle will form a perfect 'V'. This fact must always be the basis of your sighting for the double.

Only practice can teach you this, and it is only by trial and error that you will eventually get the hang of it. I cannot

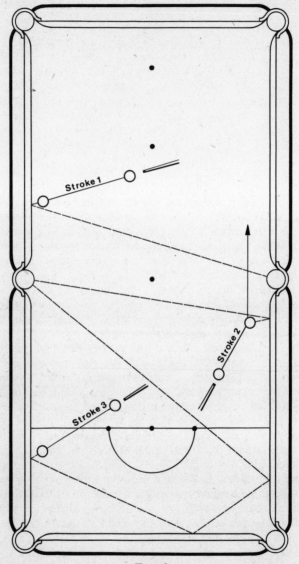

Fig. 18

help you with this other than to give you one or two ideas about how best to approach it.

There are various types of doubles, of course, but the main one is undoubtedly the double into the middle pocket when the object ball is reasonably close to the opposite side cushion (as in stroke 1 in Fig. 18). It often helps with the sighting of this stroke to stand at the middle pocket concerned and visualize the path of the object ball in reverse, noting the point of contact that has to be made on the cushion. The cue ball has then to be played on to the object ball in order to make it follow this line.

Strokes 2 and 3 in Fig. 18 show various other types of doubles which can be played. Bear in mind that corner-pocket doubles are the more risky to attempt. For one thing, you are playing into a partly closed pocket, and in the event of missing the pot there is the great risk of leaving the ball 'on' for your opponent. This is a stroke I seldom favour myself. I much prefer to play the 'cocked-hat' double into the middle pocket, which gives a greater margin of safety in the event of an unsuccessful stroke.

At all times, and even with the double, it is important to ensure that the cue ball is played into a favourable position for the next stroke.

21

Breaking Up the Reds

Making a break at snooker, apart from potting accuracy and obtaining the necessary positions to make the pots fairly simple, depends entirely on the lie of the balls. They are not always conveniently placed for making good positional moves, for the reds may be in unpottable positions. After all, you start the game with fifteen reds and it is obvious from their original placing in the triangle at the top end of the table that they will tend to bunch together, leaving no clear passage to a pocket.

This generally happens in the early stages before the pack has been greatly disturbed, but it can happen at any stage of the game, for when only one or two reds are left they might well be awkwardly placed. At first sight this would indicate the end of a break and call for a safety stroke. This, of course, is the easy way out, but if everyone adopted this attitude there would be very few big breaks.

The more expert player will look around for ways and means of forcing an opening. This can often be done by knocking the reds into position when potting a colour.

In other words as the colour is potted the cue ball is made to cannon into the reds in order to split them up.

Often a red will need only a gentle nudge to move it into a more favourable position. You must get used to looking for these opportunities.

At other times it will call for a much more forceful shot,

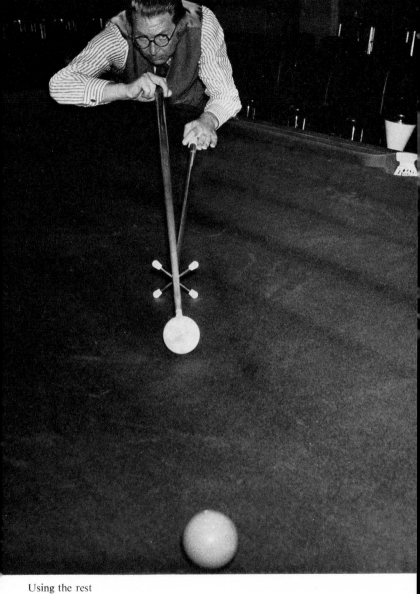

Using the rest

The swerve

when, for instance, the reds are tightly bunched, and there are lots of them. In these cases you can only hope that as many reds as possible will be favourably displaced, for when several balls are moved it is difficult to judge exactly how they will kiss into each other. Generally you will find that you have forced at least one opening which will enable you to continue your break.

I have dealt with the disturbing of the reds, but this type of play can also be utilized for cannoning a colour into a more favourable position when potting a red, or even in the later stages of a game when only the colours are on the table. Here, though, it is far more difficult, for your opportunities are more restricted.

However, let us return to breaking up a large pack of reds. If most of the triangle is still complete it makes a fairly large target from almost any position on the table.

The black, however, when being potted from its spot, offers the easiest opportunity of splitting the pack, as will be seen from the two strokes in the accompanying diagram (Fig. 19). According to the position of the cue ball you can either screw off the black directly into the pack, or, if the pot is at another angle, send the cue ball on to the top cushion and then into the pack. The stroke must be played at speed in order to displace as many reds as possible. It is no good playing a soft shot, or you would be bound to leave the cue ball bottled up.

The blue can also be used to good effect for this purpose, but once again it must be played at speed. As you will see from the diagram, the path of the cue ball is via the side and top cushions into the top of the pack. I find it is always advisable to split the pack from the top, as this tends to push the reds down the table slightly, leaving the top area clear for potting the black off its spot. However, there are many different ways of making these pack-splitting cannons, and it is up to you to study the lie of the balls and appraise the situation before making your decision.

The one thing to remember when playing this type of stroke is to make quite sure of potting the colour. It would

G

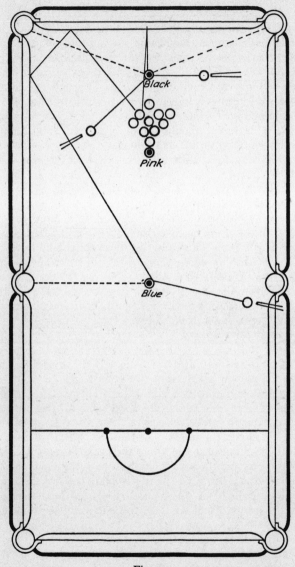

Fig. 19

be a catastrophe to miss the pot and split the reds nicely, leaving it all set up for your opponent.

For the beginner it is not easy to have one's attention divided between potting and positional play. Two-fold shots often lead to failure in one or the other. However, you have to learn to overcome this if you are to get anywhere, for every stroke in the game—not only breaking up the reds—should have a double purpose. You have to be able to pot and get position, too, if you want to make breaks.

22

More Positional Cannons

In the previous chapter I dealt mainly with the use of the cannon to break up the reds, whilst potting your colour in order to keep the break going. I was dealing generally with the situation when there are quite a number of reds on the table, as at the beginning of a game.

I also mentioned that the cannon could be usefully employed in dealing with balls that were awkwardly placed, and I feel that I should now enlarge on this aspect.

Often, if a break is to be continued, the last couple of reds may have to be moved from a bad lie on or near a cushion, or doubled. Kissing it out into the open calls for a far more delicately executed stroke than the breaking up of the pack of reds, where it is merely necessary to send the cue ball into them at speed. For one thing the target is much smaller, and a ball lying against a cushion, if hit at any speed, will fly off the cushion and give little opportunity for control. It could, in fact, finish almost anywhere.

Thus, to have any chance of success you must play a carefully calculated stroke to kiss the ball into a desired position.

Let me give you some examples of what I mean with the diagram (Fig. 20). Stroke 1 shows the last red tight on the cushion, about a foot from the middle pocket. In potting the previous red the striker elected to get on the blue, a position which he duly obtained. To continue further he must, in potting the blue, nudge that red out from the cushion. To do this he must pot the blue into the middle

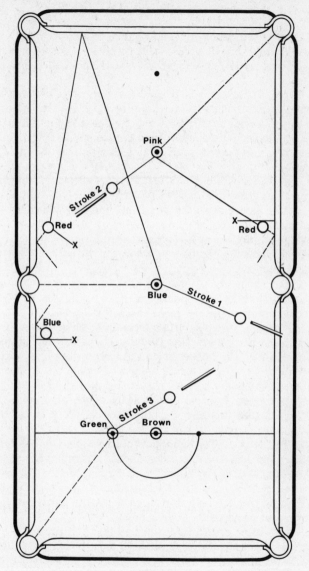

Fig. 20

pocket, at the same time sending the cue ball on to the top cushion and then down the table gently to kiss the red into position over the middle pocket. He is now well placed to continue his break.

Stroke 2 shows an alternative method of achieving the same objective as stroke 1. This time the player has got on to the pink with the previous red. He pots the pink into the corner pocket and applies stun to the cue ball so that it pulls across to kiss the red, once again leaving it over the middle pocket.

You will find similar positions constantly occurring, so practising these strokes is well worthwhile. They might look difficult, indeed they are not easy, but they are essential to break-building for good snooker is not dependent on potting ability alone. It is the ability to force these openings which makes the big difference between the ordinary player and the expert.

There are plenty of amateurs who can pot with uncanny accuracy, but few have much idea of controlling the cue ball sufficiently to make the game easier for themselves.

In stroke 3 I give one further instance of using the cannon, this time when clearing the colours. The striker has potted the yellow and is on the green. The brown is on its spot, well placed, but the blue is badly placed on the side cushion. Obviously, then, the blue has to be moved if the table is to be cleared. In order to do this the player, when potting the green into the corner pocket, screws the cue ball on to the blue, kissing it over the middle pocket. At the same time he leaves the cue ball nicely on the brown.

Here he has been looking ahead, choosing the right opportunity to make his cannon. Remember that it does not necessarily have to be left to the stroke immediately before playing the blue. In this case it is the potting of the green that provides the right moment.

Set up some of these positions so that you can try them out for yourself. They are essential aids to break-building and with practice you will be surprised at how often they can be achieved.

Practice is the key to success in snooker. You must always be experimenting with different strokes, as only in this way can you learn to face them with confidence when the positions crop up in a game.

23

Looking Ahead

At this stage I would once again stress the advisability of looking ahead when playing snooker. You should never play any stroke without having first thought about it and formed a plan of campaign.

I know that many ordinary players are content merely to pot a red and a colour, and while they adopt that attitude they will never be more than ordinary players. You must have some ambition, even if it is to make your first twenty break, and, when you have achieved that aim, for thirty and so on. The more you make, the greater the satisfaction of something achieved.

That is why I say you must plan ahead. A little bit of thought at the beginning often makes the difference between compiling a nice break or merely potting a couple of balls.

Many people think that we professional players plan a complete break before potting the first red. This is far from true, although we can often see the possibilities of a big break from the lie of the balls.

It is essential, however, to be at least two strokes ahead if the game is to be made as easy as possible. To put it plainly, you must decide on the next red before you pot the first one.

My diagram (Fig. 21) will help to explain what I mean by this. From the position shown, the 'one-shot-ahead' player will immediately see an easy red and black on, and will proceed to pot the red, stunning the cue ball so that it stops dead into the position previously occupied by the red.

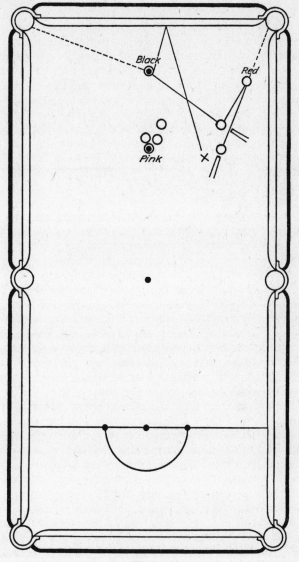

Fig. 21

Nicely on the black, it is true, but what about the next red? From this angle it is practically impossible to get into the desired position (marked X) for a nice position on the next red, and all the player will have scored is a red and a black.

Now let us look at the position again through the eyes of the player who is looking ahead, and see the other possibilities. He will play it in this fashion. First pot the red with a little screw applied to the cue ball so that it comes back into the position shown. From this angle on the black it is comparatively simple to get into position 'X' via the top cushion by stunning the cue ball slightly when the black is potted. Thus position is maintained to continue the break.

Positional play is the big secret of break-building and to get those positions you have to plan ahead and control the cue ball. It is no good letting it run wildly, for you will soon be in a hopeless mess. What is more, rigid control and good position can add much to the enjoyment of the game.

Now let us turn to another phase of looking ahead, the question of alternative strokes. Frequently when going to the table you are faced with several alternative possibilities. Indeed, it is seldom that you are left with only one possible stroke to play. Usually you can choose any of three or four different strokes, and in many cases there are often several different ways of playing the same stroke. The problem, then, is which to choose for the best.

The answer, of course, depends to a large extent on the player. Most of you will have developed your own favourite stroke, a type of shot which you know you can play successfully, and this will obviously have a big influence on your decision. You should, however, study the table well before going for your pet stroke. Perhaps there is some other move which will pay even bigger dividends?

Sometimes by attempting a stroke that is perhaps a little more difficult you may well open up the way for a break. This, then, is the shot you should choose. As I have emphasized previously, break-building is a matter of planning ahead. You have to weigh up the prospects. So don't rush

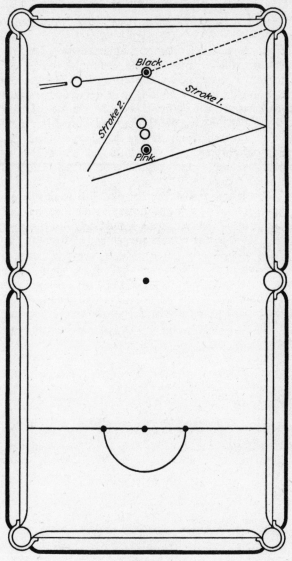

Fig. 22

into the first shot that offers itself. Give everything due consideration.

While there is often more than one way of playing a particular stroke, it is usually the position of the other balls which help you to decide on your method of play. Sometimes, however, there is nothing to prevent you from playing the stroke as you will. When it becomes a matter of personal choice I usually choose the shorter and more direct method.

For instance, the diagram (Fig. 22) shows two alternative methods of potting the black off its spot and getting on to the last two reds, which can only be potted into the top right-hand pocket.

Stroke 1 is a perfectly simple stroke with no side necessary on the cue ball. The angle of the pot is such that the cue ball will travel on to the side cushion and back into the position marked 'X' with the correct judgement of strength.

Stroke 2 shows the same position being achieved with screw being applied to the cue ball. Here again, the only concern is to play the stroke of sufficient strength to stop the cue ball in position 'X'.

Of the two I would always favour the second method, as this is the more direct. But it is largely a matter of personal choice.

24

The Ideal Pot

Whilst I am travelling the country playing exhibitions I am often asked what my favourite stroke is. I find this question difficult to answer, but on giving the matter some thought I have come to the conclusion that it is a straightish 'pot' into a corner pocket, played with stun or screw. This of course, inevitably leads to the further question: why?

The reasons for my choice are these: with a pot that is practically straight, one has the cue ball, object ball and pocket more or less in line. This is obviously much easier to sight than, for instance, a fine cut.

Secondly, with the balls in this position it is possible to stun or screw the cue ball off at practically any desired angle, which is, of course, an advantage for positioning for the next stroke.

Thirdly, I always feel more confident when playing with stun or screw, as with these strokes one gets the feeling that the cue ball is always held on course. It skids, rather than rolls, to the object ball, and there is no possibility of it 'rolling off'.

Finally, I always favour potting into a corner pocket rather than a middle, and wherever possible I always position myself for a pot into the corner. This is because I find it easier to sight a pot into this pocket. It is a point where two straight lines converge at right-angles to each other. I prefer it to the middle pocket, which is a point on a straight line.

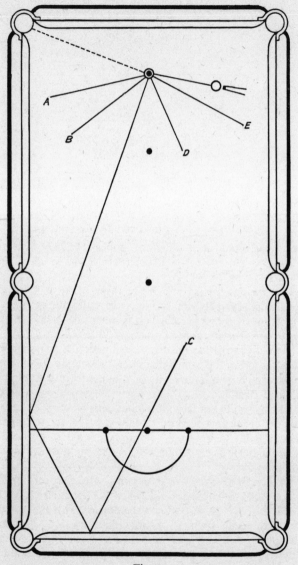

Fig. 23

What, then, does all this add up to? It is this: the ideal pot is the one that is slightly off straight. The dead-straight pot is easy to sight, but one can only send the cue ball forward towards the pocket or back on the straight line, which obviously limits the position and possibilities for the next stroke. At the other end of the scale the fine cut has the double disadvantage of being difficult to sight and, because of the fineness of contact between the cue ball and object ball, the great difficulty of controlling the cue ball for the next stroke.

My diagram (Fig. 23) shows what can be achieved from the nearly straight pot. The dotted lines coming off the object ball show some of the angles that the cue ball can be made to take after potting: from the plain-ball follow-through 'A' to the deep screw 'E'. Any of these lines can be extended (as shown at 'C'), so that from this stroke it is possible to place the cue ball practically anywhere on the table for the next stroke.

25

Selecting a Cue

I am often asked if we professionals use a special type of cue, and also to recommend what type of cue to buy.

Let me say straight away that there is nothing special about a cue. I am a firm believer in not paying too much attention to it. I believe that any cue is a good cue provided you get used to it and can play well with it. Use the same cue all the time. If it suits you, then for you it is a good cue. Whether it is worth 50p of five pounds is of no importance. The important thing it to use the same cue all the time so that you get to know the exact weight and feel of it, and it almost becomes part of you. If you keep chopping and changing your cue then your touch must necessarily suffer.

As to the weight of a cue, this varies slightly and is not necessarily of great importance provided once again that you get used to it. The average weight of a cue is sixteen and a half to seventeen ounces. Anything below or above that may still be all right, it is merely a question of individual taste.

The standard length of a cue is four feet ten and a half inches, which all professional players, without exception, find a little too long. They prefer one that is just a little shorter, as this makes it more manageable; a little more compact. Obviously the length of a cue is important. Going to the extremes we would find it difficult to play with the half-butt. Nor could we use a cue that was only two feet long. Even though I have a reasonably long reach, I use a cue which is about an inch and a half shorter than the standard length.

Contrary to popular belief, the cue need not be perfectly straight. Because a cue is slightly bent it does not prevent you from hitting the ball straight. However, obviously, if a cue is terribly bowed then it will affect your sighting.

I can speak on this subject with authority, for my own cue is like a donkey's hind-leg. Yet it has made no difference to me.

Far too much stress is laid on having a straight cue. A parallel may be drawn with the professional golfer who favours an old hickory-shafted putter which he has used since he was a lad. It is probably as twisted as it could be, but he prefers it, knowing that it will not prevent him from getting those long putts from the edge of the green.

Ninety per cent of cues in use today are made from kiln-dried wood, and it is possible that some may warp slightly. Don't blame the sports shop that supplied it, or the manufacturer. Unfortunately, the stocks of naturally seasoned wood were sadly depleted during the war and have since been in very short supply. This is a legacy we have to bear.

However, if you still feel a straight cue is most desirable, a simple test when buying one is to roll it over a flat surface. If it is made of ash, as most are nowadays, the grain should run straight, with no knots at all, and the cue should taper from butt to tip.

I have been using my cue since I played in the Boys' Billiards Championship at the age of fifteen, and there is quite a story attached to it. I travelled from my home in Exeter to Burroughes Hall, London, on Boxing Day 1938. It was to have been a through train and an uncle was to meet me at Waterloo Station. However, the schedule was altered and I had to change trains at Basingstoke. I jumped up, put on my overcoat, grabbed my suitcase and made a dash for the connection. In my panic I did not realize that I had left my cue behind until I was well on my way.

I was only fifteen and naturally very distressed. Although

H

I went to the Lost Property Office at Waterloo, I never got that cue back.

Eventually I arrived for the championship minus my cue. I was terribly upset, but Mr. Coxon, the managing director of Burroughes and Watts, told me not to worry and took me into a room where there was a table with hundreds of cues lying on it. They ranged from cheap ones to the very expensive. He told me to select one that I felt I could play with and use it during the championship, which I did.

After the championship Burroughes gave me the cue and I am still using it to this day. It has become part and parcel of me and I would feel lost without it.

The most important part of the cue is the tip. Always see that yours is of the best possible quality, and above all see that you keep it in good condition. A little care and attention can prevent a lot of the miscuing that is often blamed on to the quality of the tip.

Chalking and hitting a hard ball will eventually produce a layer of compressed chalk on top of the tip which obviously leads to miscueing when using side or screw. It is advisable occasionally to remove this hard surface in the following manner. Take a smooth file and press it over the top of the tip two or three times. Don't file it; just press it over the tip. This will crack off the compressed layer of chalk so that you are once again down to the leather. Under no circumstances use a sandpaper for this purpose, as this will cause unnecessary wear.

A file is the most suitable tool, but I emphasize again only press it on to the tip, don't file it.

Unfortunately, tips wear out and occasionally have to be renewed. This presents another problem. One obviously gets used to the feel of a particular tip and, although its resilience diminishes as it wears, this is so gradual as to be unnoticeable. By the time it reaches the end of its useful life, however, and has to be taken off, the leather has become compressed to such a degree that its 'feel' is by now entirely different from what it was when it was new. So in putting on a new tip we are faced with the problem of having immediately to get used to a tip with an entirely different 'feel'. This, unfortunately, cannot be avoided. All one can do is to always use the same type of tip to get some measure of consistency. I find that it takes me several days to get used to a new tip. For this reason I would never dream of changing it before an important match.

Whilst we are on the subject of re-tipping I recommend that you use a cue that has a brass ferrule at the tip end. This not only prevents the possibility of the cue splitting but is also an invaluable aid to re-tipping. In removing the old tip this thin circle of brass around the edge of the cue ensures that you maintain a perfectly flat surface on which to fix your new tip.

Finally a word of advice on chalking. It is quite unnecessary to screw the chalk round and round the tip for minutes on end. Too much chalk is as bad as not enough. Provided your tip is maintained in good condition a light brushing of the chalk over the tip is sufficient.

26

The Importance of Practice

Having dealt with the various phases of snooker, I am now going to return to the question of practice. I cannot over-emphasize the importance of this—you know the old saying as well as I do: 'Practice makes perfect'.

No one, no matter how efficient he is, can expect to maintain consistent form without practice. If I leave off playing for more than a few days I feel completely rusty. I start to miss pots, or I find that something is wrong with my positional play, and this means that I have to get down to the task of polishing up my strokes before I can consider playing a match. This is true of all professional players, so you can rest assured it affects the ordinary club players as well. You cannot expect to go to the table whenever you like and bang the balls down as if you have some form of radar control.

What, then, is the best method of practice? Many players think that it is merely setting the balls up and playing frames of snooker on your own. I certainly do not recommend this. In fact I would say it is completely wrong.

There is only one proper way to practise and that is to break the game down into its various components and practise each separately. After all, if you play a frame of snooker you are not likely to be faced with every type of situation. In fact you may only get one or two shots of the type that involves your particular weakness, perhaps none at all. Every game of snooker does not follow exactly the same pattern. It is only over a period of games that you can expect to experience all aspects of the game.

This is why you must break the game down and practise each phase individually. Spend some time at each until you have achieved consistency.

Whatever reason a player may have for practising, whether it be loss of form, to tune up for an important match or merely the natural desire to improve his game, the method is more or less the same.

All players, even the professionals, suffer periods of being off form or out of touch, and usually this can be traced to a particular weakness. They are doing something wrongly and their aim must be to discover exactly what this is and then to rectify it.

Remember how at the start of this book I mentioned that the big difference between the professional and the amateur is that the professional knows the reason why a ball reacts in a certain way? He has learned this by many hours of studious practice at individual shots.

A professional, naturally, cannot afford to be off form, and he gets back to the practice table just as often as he can. He cannot wait for a fault to iron itself out on its own. Although it is possible for faults to rectify themselves without the player knowing why. But this usually takes too long.

More often than not these off-form periods are due to a faulty cue action or a discrepancy in the stance. You may not be standing correctly, or you may unconsciously be pulling your head up on the stroke. Of course, the missing of an easy pot may be due to over-confidence, or from being so anxious that your action loses its smoothness.

It is therefore advisable to go back to the A B C and check that no bad habits have been creeping in.

Make sure that you are standing correctly . . . nicely balanced with feet comfortably apart, weight evenly distributed and the body perfectly poised. Check that you have no movement on the stroke, except that of the striking arm. See that you are sighting correctly and keeping your head down; that your cue action is smooth with the cue running

straight and horizontal to the bed of the table. Make sure
that you are following through and not merely jabbing at
the ball. Any bad habits that may have been developed are
almost certain to be traced.

I am sorry to have to repeat all this, but I cannot lay
sufficient stress on these fundamentals. In their anxiety to
get on too many players gloss over the basic fundamentals.
You cannot check them too often.

In order to find out if you are cueing correctly I suggest
you try stroke 1 in Fig. 24. This is the long in-off at billiards.
It is an excellent stroke for loosening up the cue action and
making sure that you are following through correctly, for
the shot can only be achieved consistently if this is so.

Ten minutes at this will really get your cue arm back into
the groove. Once you are satisfied that this is so, you are
ready for the next stage. This will depend on the player
concerned.

While playing, you should always be analysing your own
play. By doing this it is possible to pin-point weaknesses.
There will inevitably be, from time to time, certain strokes
that you miss consistently. Because of having missed this
type of stroke once or twice you naturally become frightened
of it. It is your 'bogey'.

The only way to conquer this is by playing the shot over
and over again until you find out exactly what you are doing
wrongly. Once you have discovered the reason, make the
necessary adjustments. After a while you will find that you
are able to bring the shot off and then have no further fears.
Once you overcome a 'bogey' like this, you can in future
face it with confidence.

Stroke 2 in Fig. 24 shows a method which I use myself
for potting and positional practice. Place the black on its
spot with the cue ball in the position shown, slightly off
straight. The object of this exercise is to pot the black and
regain position on it either by stunning on to the top
cushion and back into the same position (shown by line
'A') or by following through on to the top cushion (as in
'B') to get on the black into the opposite corner pocket.

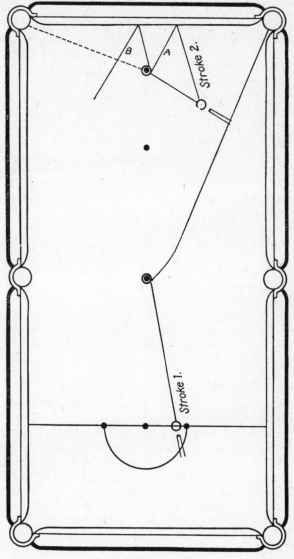

Fig. 24

After each successful pot re-spot the black and continue. If you can do this five times consecutively you are doing well.

MORE ON PRACTICE

Although I have pointed out the importance of practice, I am against being a slave to it. It is purely my own idea—and I don't have to be right—but I consider it is useless to force anyone, or for anyone to force themselves, to practise any game for a specific time. In other words, I think it is the wrong approach to lay down a practice programme and stick rigidly to it.

Practice will only do you good if you are getting stuck into it 100 per cent, and really concentrating on what you are doing.

If you are forcing yourself to practise when you are not in the mood it can do more harm than good. Therefore I recommend that you break off when you get a little tired and do something entirely different.

During my years of intensive practice, when I first decided to join the professional ranks, I used to put my cue down and go out and mow the lawn, push a roller up and down, anything to take my mind off snooker for a while. Then, mentally refreshed, back I would go to it again.

PRACTICE ON A SMALL TABLE

Unfortunately, the accurate, exacting conditions of a full-size billiards table cannot be reproduced in miniature. The proud possessor of a small home table, therefore, will find himself at a disadvantage whenever he plays on the larger table. The angles from the cushions will be different, and some of the spots will be of such long range that the player will feel that he is performing on a ten-acre field. On the small table, by comparison the balls are bigger, and this, added to the more confined area, tends to create congestion of the balls to such an extent that it becomes extremely difficult to manœuvre the cue ball into position.

There is one aspect of the game that does remain the

same, however, the A B C. The stance, bridge, holding of the cue and cue action can all be learned just as effectively on the small table as on the full-sized, and for this reason the facility of a home table can be of invaluable aid to the beginner.

I do not decry the miniature table. It can afford a great deal of interest and amusement to the household, particularly to the younger members. After all, there are very few homes today that are large enough to house a full-sized table.

27

Temperament

Temperament plays a big part in snooker, as it does in every other game. It is difficult to define exactly the ideal temperament for a ball game, and there are conflicting ideas about this. However, I am convinced that you must have the type of temperament whereby you will get annoyed with yourself when you are not doing as well as you should. Personally, I find that this stimulates me to do better.

A complacent person, who is playing badly, is likely to accept it with a shrug of his shoulders. He will tend to say: 'Well, I'm not doing so well today,' and let it go at that. He will naturally fall by the wayside.

The player who gets annoyed with himself, however, will tend to force himself to play better by sheer grit and determination. His very nature will drive him on to greater efforts, making him the player most likely to pull himself together, in moments of crisis, to go on and win. I am sure that only such a person can be a champion.

Snooker demands calculated concentration, every shot has to be carefully and deliberately thought out before it is played, and the mind must at all times be focussed completely on the game, even when one's opponent is in play. The stress and strain that is endured during a closely fought match is terrific.

Being subjected to this for such long periods can often make a player over-tense, so that his muscles tighten up to such an extent that he is unable to produce the quality of play to which he is accustomed. At these times his little show of annoyance, as well as spurring him on to greater efforts, acts also as a safety-valve, allowing him to 'blow off a little steam' so that he may readjust himself to the necessary degree of tension.

In order to play this or any other ball game to the best of our ability the mind must be keyed to the extent where all else is excluded, whilst the body is physically relaxed. This is a difficult state to achieve, as the keying of the mind will often lead to tensing of the muscles. When it is achieved, then, and only then, will a player give of his best.

This brings to mind an amusing incident that occurred when I was playing Fred Davis in the *News of the World* tournament at Leicester Square Hall. It was a particularly important match because the position of the tournament was such that both Fred and I were in a position to win the top prize, both having done well in our preceding heats.

We had reached a critical stage of the match and I kept on making silly mistakes. The fact is, I was getting into a hopeless tangle, while Fred was getting away with it.

Then came a wonderful opportunity. But in a couple of strokes I once again got into a mess, took a chance, missed and left Fred on with what looked a certain sixty or seventy break. I was so annoyed with myself that I stormed out through the swing doors, into the manager's office and proceeded to let off steam.

We had a system there whereby the referee rang a buzzer to recall any player who had left the room should his opponent break down. I had not been more than a few minutes telling Ted Lowe, the manager and a very dear friend of mine, what a stupid idiot I had been, when the buzzer went.

My immediate reaction was 'Crikey, he's missed it; I'm in again,' and I went bouncing back into the hall to be greeted by a tremendous burst of laughter. Fred had left me with a most impossible position . . . the cue ball jammed right up behind the brown, while at the top of the table there were about eight or nine reds all nicely split up. I was so completely snookered that whatever I played, whether I hit a red or not, I must almost certainly leave an easy red for Fred. I did, and he proceeded to step in and win the game.

This was the game before the interval and as we made our way to the dressing room for a ten-minute break I asked Fred the reason for all the laughter. He explained. 'You know you were getting a little irate with yourself at having let me in, and it was obvious that you were thoroughly fed-up by the way you bounced out. I failed to take full advantage of the leave, and was so tangled up after three or four shots that I dribbled up behind the brown to leave the snooker. As I went to my seat I just remarked: "Fasten your safety-belts," and everyone saw the funny side of it.' I did too, and joined in the laughter, though I must confess I hadn't appreciated it much at the time.

I know that it is essential for me to get that way at times; for some people it would perhaps be disastrous. It depends entirely on one's temperament.

This attitude at the table is completely opposite to my nature, for I am normally a very easy-going person. But at the table I can get really vicious.

Joe Davis was also like this. He would get furious with himself at times, when things were not going to his liking, and his reactions would be much the same as mine—he would give himself a good talking to, then return determined to do a lot better.

Fred Davis has a very good temperament and appears to be very easy-going. But he is affected in exactly the same way as the rest of us. The only difference with Fred is that he has a remarkable facility for not showing it, and is able to put on a smiling countenance. But underneath this cloak he too, at times, gets very wild with himself.

John Spencer and Ray Reardon, the best of the New Wave of professionals who came into the game in the late 1960's, both have excellent temperaments. Spencer, outwardly very casual and easy-going, seeming to take everything completely in his stride, betrays his nervous tension by the odd cough and sniff. Without this escape valve he might well go beyond the desirable state of being keyed up into the dangerous state of becoming over-tense.

Reardon, however, appears to have no particular mannerism to reveal to even the most discerning that he is suffering any undue pressure and, like all champions, seems to maintain the ability to think clearly, stay cool and do the right thing whatever the state of the game. No doubt he still suffers from the tensions of the game—he just doesn't show it.

If Joe, Fred, John, Ray and myself, all winners of the World Championship, are affected in this way, it would seem to indicate that this is what creates the ability to pull out that little extra when it is most needed. In fact I believe that most top-class players at others sports are affected similarly. It may be that this is that little extra undefined 'something' that is necessary to make a champion.

To avoid any possible confusion let me explain here and now that this ruthlessness, this aggression, is nothing to do with bad sportsmanship or the mere fact of winning or losing. This occasional annoyance is always directed at oneself, never at one's opponent, and stems from the pursuit of absolute perfection. The professional player sets himself an extremely high standard and he is seldom, if ever, satisfied with his performance. His self-criticism is so severe that even when he has acquitted himself brilliantly he will still remember the few strokes that didn't quite come off.

What, then, are the lessons to be learned from all this.

1. Try to develop a fighting instinct, so that no matter what the odds, given the slightest opportunity, you can always be likely to turn the tables on your opponent.
2. Condition your mind to concentrating 100 per cent on the game, whilst being physically relaxed.
3. Strive for perfection at all times. You won't achieve it, nobody ever has, but it provides the spur that must lead to improvement.

28

Wearing Spectacles

Keen eyesight is an obvious advantage to a snooker-player, and for a long time it was thought that only those so blessed could become first-class players. This has been proved incorrect, for both Fred Davis and myself wear glasses, but let me state right away that only the myopic, or short-sighted, person can hope to do this successfully. This particular defect of sight is corrected with lenses that sharpen up the blurred distance without affecting the near vision so that the sight is normal over all distances.

At the other end of the scale, however, lenses made for correction at reading distance are of no use for any other purpose, hence bi-focal lenses. A player with this type of eyesight would need constant changes of glasses for different-range shots, which, of course, is impracticable.

Contact or corneal lenses are the obvious answer, if you can wear them, as these correct the vision without any added encumbrances. Unfortunately some people cannot get used to them, and there will be others who are unable to afford them. For you, a specially adapted frame for glasses can be of great help.

Both Fred Davis and myself were forced to wear glasses before contact lenses were perfected and we have to thank Fred for pioneering the specially adapted frame. He had to take to glasses before the war, and was so troubled by this handicap that his career was threatened. He therefore took his problem to an occulist and between them they developed a specially adapted frame which had an extra hinge at each side so that the whole of the frame could be swivelled back against the eyebrows.

This enabled the player, when in playing position, to look through the lenses instead of over the top of the frame.

It was several years later, soon after I became a professional, that I had to resort to glasses, and I immediately adopted the same type of frames for playing. I found it a tremendous handicap at first and it took me about a year to get used to playing in them, but knowing how Fred had prevailed I was determined to do likewise.

I have now become so used to my swivel frames that I am happy to continue with them rather than risk adjusting myself to the more modern contact lenses.

I use my special glasses only when I am playing. I have the ordinary type for normal wear. Thus I have to make certain that I always take my playing glasses with me. There was one occasion when giving an exhibition that I inadvertently left them at home. I tried to play in my ordinary glasses, but found it impossible because of looking over the top of the frame. Eventually I took them off and played without glasses. This was most difficult, for the long-range ball looked like a ball of wool, with no clearly defined outline. Fortunately, however, I played reasonably well, and amused everyone by quipping: 'It's wonderful what a good memory will do.'

29

A Professional Career in Snooker

At the beginning of this book I stated that snooker has a smaller percentage of good players than any other game, but for those who do make the grade the rewards today are immeasurably higher than they have ever been.

The tremendous impact of BBC2's Pot Black series has not only taken the game to an entirely new public but has also awakened the interest of a number of important commercial sponsors. More people are playing than ever before, albeit most of them socially rather than competitively, and the Snooker equipment firms are doing an unprecedented level of trade. Even so, facilities are still inadequate to meet demand. I foresee the establishment of a number of large scale Snooker Centres throughout the country.

All these things indirectly benefit the professional player so that today more than ever before a financial incentive exists for outstanding young players.

It was different when I turned professional. Then, unless one was sponsored, or had private means, there was little chance of reaching the top for it was practically impossible to earn a living with your cue in those early years.

I was very fortunate. Joe Davis encouraged me to become a professional, and it was a great friend of his, and mine, the late Bill Lampard, a Bristol baker and confectioner, and a great enthusiast of the game, who became my sponsor. I went to live with him at Bristol, where he had a special billiards room built on to his house for my use. It was there that I knuckled down to the task of learning the game.

In my young days in the profession I was fortunate, too, in that I never missed an opportunity of doing well. Yet it took me five or six years to even begin to make a name for myself in the professional ranks.

In my first season the *Sunday Empire News* sponsored a tournament with £1,000 in prize-money. It was run in two sections. Four players—Joe Davis, Fred Davis, Sidney Smith and Walter Donaldson—were invited to play in the competition proper. The remainder, which included me, had to play a qualifying section. In the qualifying section everyone played off the same mark, but the competition proper was on a double-handicap basis. In addition to the normal handicapping of each match there was also a sealed handicap of frames which was not revealed until after the last frame was completed.

This provided a shock in the case of the meeting of the Davis brothers, who played on level terms, for the sealed handicap revealed Fred had to give Joe two frames start. Fred had actually proved the victor by the odd frame until this revelation, which meant that he had, in fact, lost by one frame. It was a little unsatisfactory, and made something of a mockery of Fred's victory. It has never been tried since.

But back to my position. I was fortunate enough to win the qualifying section and thus get the opportunity of my first real match play against the four finest snooker-players in the world. Aided by a generous handicap, I was able to finish runner-up to Joe, and out of that £1,000 prize-money I collected £400, just £50 less than Joe, the winner.

I received £250 for finishing second and another £150 for winning the qualifying section.

My success in this event was to have a big influence on my future career, for the following year when the *News of the World* introduced their £1,500 Professional Snooker Tournament I was invited straight into the competition proper. I had taken my chance and was now in the big-time game.

The *News of the World* tournament ran for some ten

years, during which time I twice won the first prize and was twice runner-up. The competition against the best players in the world proved invaluable to me.

As in everything else, you have to take your chances when offered.

Unfortunately, the closing of Leicester Square Hall, the Mecca of the professional game for 60 years, and the retirement of Joe Davis signalled a decline in the professional game which caused the premature retirement of several leading players. There were no tournaments though there was still a living to be made from playing exhibitions in clubs.

This situation persisted until as a result of my exhibition tours sponsored by John Player and Co, I persuaded the company to sponsor the World Professional Championship. The first time the Championship was held under their banner, in 1968, I defended the title successfully against Eddie Charlton, the Australian champion, but the following year my ten-year reign ended with my defeat by John Spencer. In 1970, I was within an ace of regaining the title when I caught up from 15 frames down to only one down against Ray Reardon before eventually losing 39–34.

30

The Rules

Interpretation of the rules of snooker leads to more arguments than in most other games. One of the reasons for this is that few people ever read them, and most players tend to base their knowledge on local traditions that have been handed on.

The rules are the copyright of the Billiards and Snooker Control Council and their publication is somewhat restricted. This could well be why they are not more widely known.

You will find a set of the rules hanging in most billiards rooms, but how many of you have ever stopped to study them? Precious few, I expect. In fact, I would say not one in a hundred.

Even when they are read, however, few people really understand them. In fact you need to be a Philadelphia lawyer to interpret them to fit any specific occasion. They are written in such a manner that you have really to delve into them to find a rule that fits a particular situation.

Generally one gets a working knowledge simply through conversancy with the game; through the experience of playing. One tends to make a note of the various rules as they crop up, but this is often insufficient to cope with the many intricate problems that can occur.

The rules are made to govern the game that is being refereed, where the onus of claiming fouls and stating what must or must not be done rests on a third person. The biggest percentage of games, however, are played without referees and this often leads to complications because there is no one to decide what must happen.

The only advice I can offer is that you insist on having a competent referee whenever you are playing a game of any importance. His decisions must, of course, be strictly adhered to, and in this way the game may be played without incident. Certain types of fouls can only be decided upon by a referee. A player may inadvertently touch a ball with his shirt-sleeve or other part of his body when getting down to his stroke. In most cases he would be unaware of this and would probably hotly deny doing so if challenged by his opponent. But if fouled by a referee he must, of course, accept it graciously.

With regard to this type of foul it is important to remember that you foul by merely touching a ball. It does not have to be moved.

WHEN DOES A GAME START?

I have been amazed at the number of people who think that when a player breaks off at snooker, and fails to hit the reds, he must take the shot again. In other words they believe that he must break the pack. This is entirely contrary to the rules. The game of snooker commences when the tip of the cue strikes the cue ball and anything that happens after that is subject to the same rules as at any other stage of the game. If the triangle of reds is completely missed, the player has committed a foul, and forfeits the corresponding number of points, in this case four, provided the cue ball has not struck a colour, in which case it would be to the value of that ball if higher than four. The next player then plays from wherever the ball has come to rest.

So remember, as soon as your cue tip strikes the ball the game is under way.

RE-SPOTTING THE COLOURS

The re-spotting of balls sometimes causes complications and arguments. To play a stroke while a colour is off the table is a foul and is penalized to the value of the offending ball, or the value of the ball on, whichever is the greater.

That sounds straightforward enough, but the trouble usually arises when several strokes have been played before it is realized that a ball is missing. What, you may ask, happens then? Some people are under the impression that the player loses the whole of a break, but this is not so. The rule is such that the foul is committed only by the last stroke played before the discovery of the error. All strokes prior to that are condoned, and the break up to then is counted. Regardless of when the omission occurs the person in play at the moment the mistake is realized is the one who is penalized.

You may think that this sounds a little harsh, but the rules clearly state that a player must always see that all balls are correctly spotted before he takes his stroke. Even though it was perhaps a referee's job to re-spot the ball, the player himself should ascertain that everything is correct before playing his stroke.

It is also a foul if a stroke is played when a colour has been placed on the wrong spot, as can easily happen with the yellow. It is quite common for a player to spot the yellow on the green spot, or vice versa, because he has become confused as to which side of the brown it should go.

We now come to the question of where a ball should be placed when its own spot is covered. For instance, a colour may be potted after it has been off its spot for some time. In the interim period a red may have covered or partially covered the spot so that the ball cannot be replaced. In this case it goes on the highest spot unoccupied; this applies to any colour that will not re-spot in its own position.

In the event of all spots being occupied the rule states that it must go as near its own spot as possible, between that spot and the nearest part of the top cushion, without touching another ball.

Let me explain this more fully by using the pink as an example. It would have to be placed as near as possible to its own spot towards the black, but it must be in the exact centre of the table. In other words it cannot go to either side of its spot but must be on a line between the pink and black spots. If, for instance, the lie of the other balls was such that it would not go anywhere there it would then go behind the black spot.

THE TOUCHING BALL

One rule of snooker which players find most difficult to interpret is that which governs the situation when the cue ball is touching another ball. At first sight the rule appears to be contradictory, but I will try to explain it as simply as possible.

The first thing to remember is that at all times the cue ball must be played away from the ball it is touching without disturbing it. If the touching ball is moved then a foul has been committed and the appropriate points are forfeited.

Now we come to the part which causes so much confusion because of appearing to contradict itself. If the cue ball is touching a red, and the player is 'on' a red, then all he need do is play away and does not need to touch another ball. By virtue of playing away from a touching ball that is 'on' he is deemed to have played a lawful stroke on that ball. If, however, he is 'on' a colour and the cue ball is touching a red he must play to hit that colour in order to play a lawful stroke. Similarly if the cue ball is touching a colour and the ball is 'on' a red he must still hit a red or pay the penalty. In each of these cases he is not deemed to have hit the touching ball.

If you look at the diagram (Fig. 25) you will see a couple of instances of the touching ball rule being applied. In stroke 1 the cue ball is touching a red when the player is in fact on a red. He elected to play a safety stroke on to the baulk cushion and by virtue of having been touching a ball 'on' is deemed to have played a fair stroke. If there had been another red that he could have potted without disturbing the red he was touching this would have been in order and the player would continue his break.

Stroke 2 shows the cue ball touching the black when the player is 'on' a red. Here he played a safety stroke off the

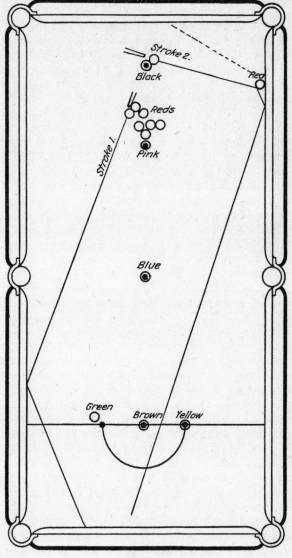

Fig. 25

red on the side cushion, this being in fact the only red he could directly hit. The difference here is that the player had to strike a red in order to make a lawful stroke. If there had been a red in a pottable position he would have been quite in order playing it as long as he did not disturb the black in doing so.

THE FREE BALL

The free-ball rule often creates controversy among club players and it is as well to get a clear understanding of this. You can claim a free ball when your opponent has committed a foul and left the cue ball in such a position that you cannot play a direct shot on to either side of the ball 'on'. In this case you nominate a ball to play. If, for instance, you are on a red and having been snookered after a foul you choose the yellow as a free ball, you can pot this and it will count as a red with a score of one. Should you, however, miss the nominated ball (in this case the yellow) and still contrive to hit a red then you will be deemed to have committed a foul, for you must strike the nominated ball first.

It is not permissible to lay a snooker, either by design or accident, behind the nominated ball. In other words, you cannot name a ball and just trickle up behind it. You can, however, play off a nominated ball to lay a snooker behind another colour.

You may also use your free ball for the purposes of a plant, to pot a ball that is 'on', provided, of course, that you hit the nominated colour first.

THE 'PLAY AGAIN' RULE

There are often occasions in a game of snooker when a player commits a foul, but despite forfeiting the appropriate penalty leaves a position that is to his distinct advantage.

Let me give you an example. Only the last two balls remain on the table and the player has gone in-off, but the balls are so placed that the black is on the brink of the pocket with the pink so close to it that any movement of the pink will send the black toppling in. To play this shot would cost seven points, the value of the black, and could well decide the game. To meet this kind of situation, and prevent a player reaping advantage from his own infringement, a new rule has been introduced whereby the next player now has the right to make his opponent play again after a foul stroke has been committed.

The rule has been in general use for some years, but in some instances is not fully understood and is often misinterpreted.

The rule was evolved some years ago by the professionals, who adopted it in their own matches for seven or eight years before it became a general rule of snooker. If used properly it is, to my mind, infallible.

Let me interpret the rule a little for you before showing you some of its practical uses.

The rule in no way affects the free-ball rule, whereby a player, finding himself snookered after a foul, may nominate any ball of his choice, such ball, for that particular stroke, becoming the same value as the ball 'on'. This still applies, and the player finding himself well placed with a free ball will, of course, take it.

There are occasions, however, when a free ball is of no use, and the player concerned is placed at a disadvantage by having to take it. Here is where the 'new' rule can be applied, for he can request his opponent to play again.

Let us turn to Fig. 26. This shows the last four colours on the table and the player has a free ball by virtue of his opponent having played a foul stroke. What is he to do? Neither the blue, pink nor black is in a convenient position for potting or for playing a snooker. Whatever shot he plays, he will most likely leave the brown 'on' for his opponent. Using the 'new' rule the answer is, of course, simple. He asks his opponent to play again, and the defaulter now has to hit the brown or forfeit the appropriate points.

The thing to remember is that the rule can be applied at any stage of the game, whether or not a free ball is involved. It may happen that a player goes in-off at the beginning of

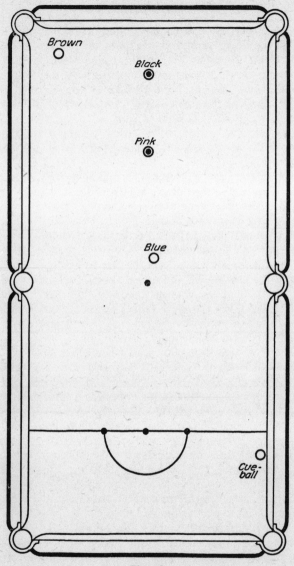

Fig. 26

a game when all fifteen reds are on the table. On placing the cue ball in the 'D' the next player finds that there is not a red he can pot, and that from the position of the balls even a safety stroke is a difficult matter. Here again he would ask his opponent to play again. In other words, he would take this step whenever he was unhappy with the position left after his opponent had fouled.

The rule also provides the answer to the player who cunningly plays a deliberate miss in order to extricate himself from a difficult position. It can often be advantageous to forfeit four points to make sure of leaving the position absolutely safe. Hitherto the referee could take drastic disciplinary action in these cases if he was convinced that the miss was deliberate. But what a difficult decision it was for him to make!

Under the 'play again' rule, however, a player cannot possibly gain an advantage from this unsportsmanlike stroke as he would be asked to play again.

POINTS OF ARGUMENT

I have often heard arguments over the question of a ball bouncing off the table and on to the rail, then running into a pocket. Many people are under the impression that this is a foul. It is not. It is quite legitimate, though I don't recommend your trying to pot this way. It is a foul, however, if the ball stays up on the rail, and it means a forfeiture of the appropriate points. Should it be the cue ball, the next player plays from the 'D' and if it is a colour it is re-spotted, while a red would be deemed to be off the table and placed in a pocket.

It is exactly the same as if the ball had been forced right off the table.

This brings me round to the question of a ball that is hovering on the edge of a pocket suddenly falling in during the next stroke without having been played. This can be caused by vibration, for even though billiards tables are solidly built, the ball that is finely balanced can move. In this case it has to be replaced and the stroke played again.

31

Conclusion

Snooker has lots of enthusiasts. They are the backbone of the game, and although they may never be great players themselves, they appreciate skill in others.

It is a fascinating game that gets a hold on you . . . just like golf. I suppose this is because it offers a constant challenge. You can never completely master it, no matter how good you become.

No one ever became so good at a ball game that they could play it like a machine. They may for eighty per cent of the time, but there is always the odd time when things are difficult. The difficulty with snooker arises from the fact that there is no pattern to it. Every game is different from the one before, and you have to knock the balls in from wherever they are lying, which is so often from the most awkward positions.

If the reds break up in a reasonable manner then a big break can be made, and this is what the majority of people like to see. Of course the big thrill to both player and spectator is to see all the twenty-one balls potted in a single break. It has been done many times. In fact I have completed such a feat twenty-eight times. My highest break is 146 made up of fourteen reds and blacks, a red and a pink, and all the colours.

The connoisseur of the game, however, the real enthusiast, is more likely to appreciate the games that are really difficult, when two professionals are engaged in a battle of wits, struggling to make an opening. It means lots of safety made over 650 century breaks. I only count those that are made in public, and I assure you that no one will ever be able to make 100 breaks to order. It is always a tremendous achievement.

There is, however, a great deal more to being a Snooker professional than simply being able to play. Snooker, particularly in exhibitions but to an increasing extent in sponsored tournaments, is part of show business. Spectators come not only to admire our skill but to be entertained. A memorable quip can win over as many fans as a superlative shot. To look at this in reverse, I need an audience in order to be able to give of my best, both verbally and on the table.

In my travels I have played on tables on which it is impossible to play one's best game though two occasions when I did manage to overcome the conditions stick in my memory. One was on a tour of South Africa when I played in a small dorp where the club had a table on which the cushions had perished to such an extent that, no matter how hard I hit the cue ball, it was impossible to get it to travel back past the blue spot!

I only took my cue out of my case at all to avoid disappointing the people who had looked forward to my visit, but lo and behold, the balls split in such a way that I managed to make a 120 break without the cue-ball touching a cushion!

On another occasion, I drove with Rex Williams through thick fog from Birmingham to the Lake District to arrive one and a half hours late and find myself playing an a table whose pockets were so small that they looked smaller than the balls!

Rex and I started off with a few minutes' billiards, which turned into a fiasco because neither of us could get the balls into the pockets. If billiards was so difficult snooker hardly seemed worth attempting but by some miracle the balls started to go in and I cleared the table with a 130 odd.

There have, of course, been times when I have felt like

a million dollars and been unable to produce any form at all. I have learnt to be philosophical about this because worrying only makes matters worse.

People who have seen me only on Pot Black imagine that a professional's life is like that all the time. It isn't. There are some big tournaments but a professional's bread and butter is still club exhibitions, travelling 20,000 miles a year, playing on all sorts of tables in all sorts of places from the lowliest village club to a millionaire's mansion.

It's a great life and I wouldn't change it though I doubt whether I will ever have a thrill like winning the Amateur Championship which I had entered as an unknown. The professional title was the result of a more prolonged build-up, a build-up which contained my most bitter disappointment when I lost to Fred Davis in the final at the Tower Circus, Blackpool, after leading from the start up to the final session.

Even in the tensest match, though, I've never stopped being myself. This I believe is one of my great secrets of success.

Enjoy yourself and good luck!